# 60
# THINGS I CAN DRAW

## *Monsters and Mythological Beasts*

by Kaye Quinn

**DERRYDALE BOOKS**
New York

This 1990 edition is published by Derrydale Books, distributed by Outlet Book Company, Inc.
a Random House Company, 225 Park Avenue South, New York, New York 10003,
by arrangement with RGA Publishing Group, Inc.

Printed and bound in the United States of America

Library of Congress Cataloging-in-Publication Data

Quinn, Kaye.
60 things I can draw, monsters / Kaye Quinn.
p.    cm.
Summary: Step-by-step instructions for drawing sixty frightening
monsters.
ISBN 0-517-03565-0
1. Monsters in art—Juvenile literature.   [1. Drawing—Technique-
-Juvenile literature.   2. Monsters in art.   3. Drawing—Technique.]
I. Title.   II. Title: Sixty things I can draw, monsters.
NC825.M6Q56   1990
743'.6—dc20        90-38299        CIP        AC

10   9   8   7   6   5   4   3   2   1

# INTRODUCTION

Drawing is fun! It can also be easy. Follow the step-by-step instructions in this book, and you will learn how to turn simple shapes such as circles, triangles, and ovals into scary-looking monsters and creepy mythological creatures. You will learn how to "build" a drawing, adding more detail at each step until your drawing looks just the way you want it to look. You will need a few simple materials to start.

**PENCILS:** It is best to start with a light pencil, so you can erase your marks easily when you add the final details. You can use pens, crayons, markers, and colored pencils to finish your drawing.

**PAPER:** Any paper will do–large, like newsprint, or small, like a piece of notebook paper.

**ERASER:** You will need a big eraser. The best kind is called a kneaded eraser–you can pull and stretch it to any size. It will pick up light pencil strokes and won't leave crumbs.

Now you are ready to begin!

# MONSTER DETAILS

Some monsters and mythological creatures have rough, scaly skin. Others have bumps and knobs on their skin. Here are four easy ways to create these textures and shadows.

Short pencil strokes in the same direction will give your creature rough or hairy-looking skin.

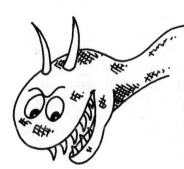

"Cross hatching" will give your creature scaly-looking skin. Make short strokes in one direction and then "cross hatch" with short strokes in the opposite direction.

Small circles and short strokes will give a bumpy look to your creature. A heavier line under each circle will make the bumps look like they're popping right off the page!

Short, curved lines will give your monster a fur coat.

3

# LET'S BEGIN!

Here are some basic instructions for drawing the creatures in this book.

Before you start to draw, look closely at the sample monster picture below. Imagine a line that runs through the center of the monster. We'll call this the "direction line." It shows the basic movement of the monster, and acts as a "hook" on which to hang all the shapes that will make your drawing easy to do.

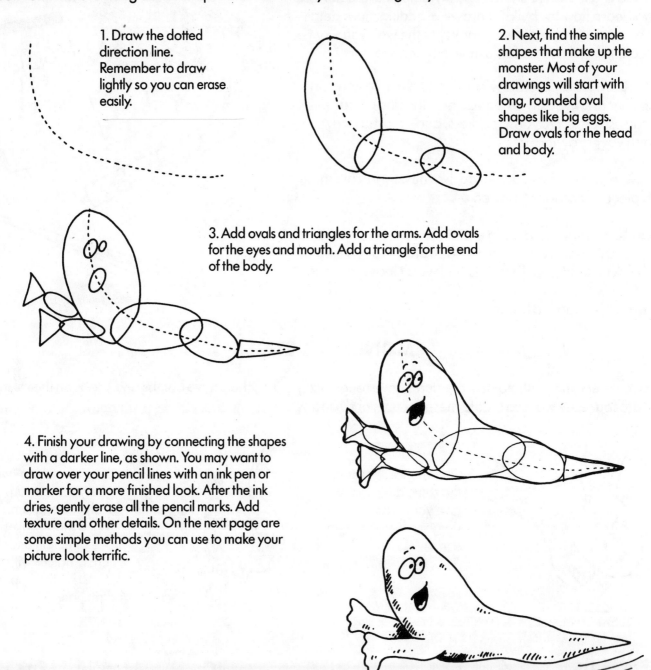

1. Draw the dotted direction line. Remember to draw lightly so you can erase easily.

2. Next, find the simple shapes that make up the monster. Most of your drawings will start with long, rounded oval shapes like big eggs. Draw ovals for the head and body.

3. Add ovals and triangles for the arms. Add ovals for the eyes and mouth. Add a triangle for the end of the body.

4. Finish your drawing by connecting the shapes with a darker line, as shown. You may want to draw over your pencil lines with an ink pen or marker for a more finished look. After the ink dries, gently erase all the pencil marks. Add texture and other details. On the next page are some simple methods you can use to make your picture look terrific.

Once you learn how to build and draw the creatures, try some ideas of your own. Draw the monsters in different poses and try putting two creatures in the same scene. You can color your creature and background any way you want. Don't worry if your monster looks different from the sample in the book — it should. That means you are showing your own style. But most of all — HAVE FUN!

# SWAMP MONSTER

Lots of stories have been written about monsters that live in bogs and swamps. Here's one covered with slime.

1. Draw the direction line. Add a large shape for the head.

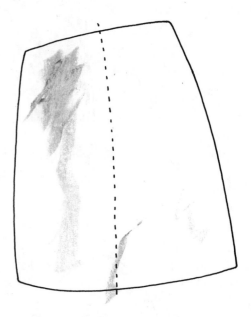

2. Draw the direction line and ovals for the eyes. Add ovals for the nose, mouth, ears, and arm. Draw lines for the fingers and the water.

3. To finish your drawing, connect the shapes and erase your guidelines. Add details to show the slime, teeth, eyes, and claws.

# GHOST ON THE RUN

This ghost must have seen a really scary monster!

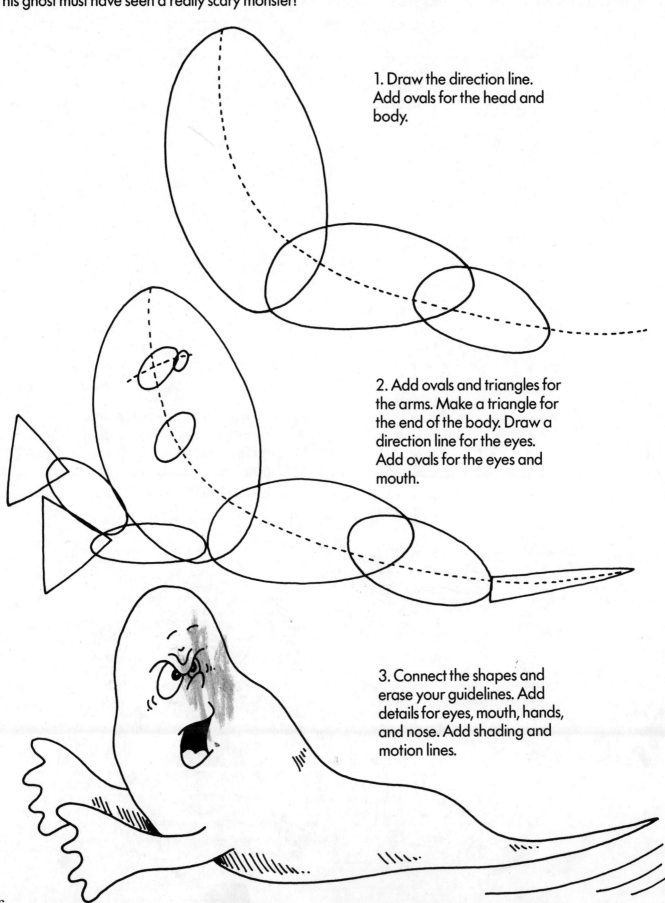

1. Draw the direction line. Add ovals for the head and body.

2. Add ovals and triangles for the arms. Make a triangle for the end of the body. Draw a direction line for the eyes. Add ovals for the eyes and mouth.

3. Connect the shapes and erase your guidelines. Add details for eyes, mouth, hands, and nose. Add shading and motion lines.

# SPACE CREATURE

Many movies and stories feature creatures from other planets. This one has a large bald head and big eyes.

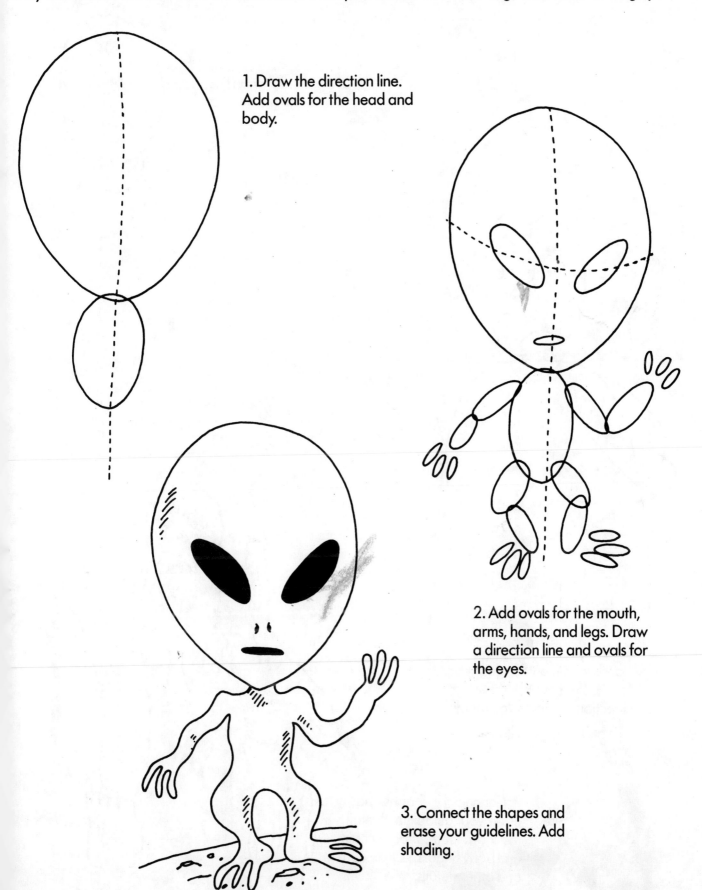

1. Draw the direction line. Add ovals for the head and body.

2. Add ovals for the mouth, arms, hands, and legs. Draw a direction line and ovals for the eyes.

3. Connect the shapes and erase your guidelines. Add shading.

# SPIRIT

Here's a spirit that's come back to haunt you. It's dressed in tatters.

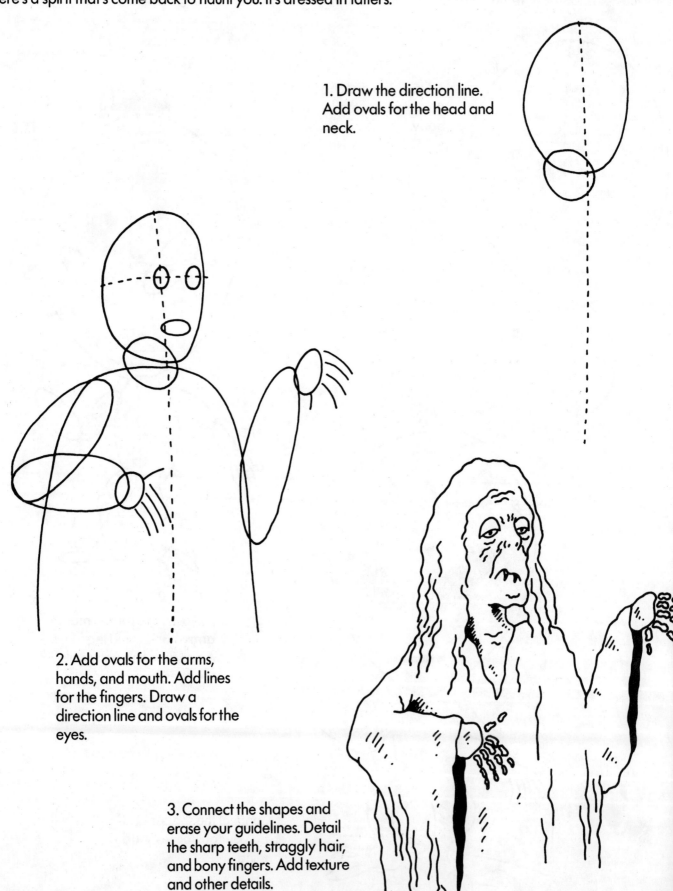

1. Draw the direction line. Add ovals for the head and neck.

2. Add ovals for the arms, hands, and mouth. Add lines for the fingers. Draw a direction line and ovals for the eyes.

3. Connect the shapes and erase your guidelines. Detail the sharp teeth, straggly hair, and bony fingers. Add texture and other details.

# SKELETON HEAD

If you add eyeballs to a skeleton head, it looks even scarier!

1. Draw two direction lines. Add ovals for the skull and jaw.

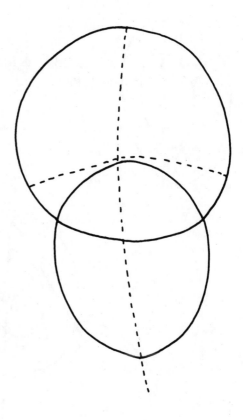

2. Add ovals for the eye sockets and neck bones. Make a shape for the mouth. Add a triangle for the nose socket.

3. Connect the shapes and erase your guidelines. Add eyeballs, teeth, shading, and other details.

9

# GHOULIE

Wrap a skeleton in a sheet to make a creepy ghoul!

1. Draw the direction line. Add ovals for the hood and face.

2. Draw a large triangle for the body. Add another direction line and ovals for the eyes and a triangle for the nose. Add ovals for the arms and hands. Draw lines for the fingers.

3. Connect the shapes and erase your guidelines. Detail teeth, eyes, and nose. Add texture.

# HERCULES BEETLE

This is a real insect that must look pretty scary to small insects! The Hercules Beetle is one of the largest and strongest of all insects.

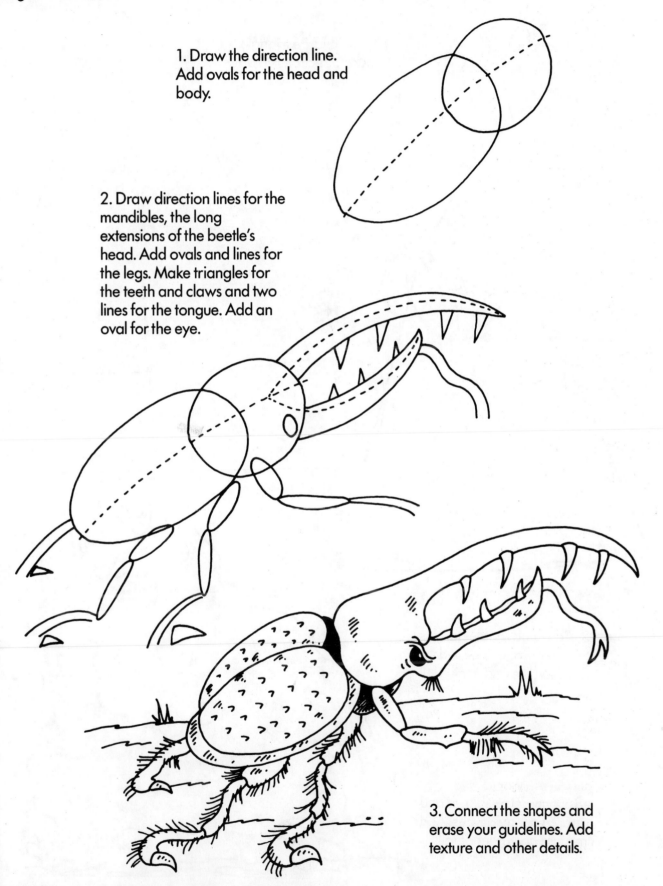

1. Draw the direction line. Add ovals for the head and body.

2. Draw direction lines for the mandibles, the long extensions of the beetle's head. Add ovals and lines for the legs. Make triangles for the teeth and claws and two lines for the tongue. Add an oval for the eye.

3. Connect the shapes and erase your guidelines. Add texture and other details.

11

# SLIME MONSTER

Start with any basic shape and add lots of curving lines to make the monster look like it's dripping and oozing.

1. Draw a large triangle. Draw a direction line down the center.

2. Add ovals for the hands, feet, head, and nose. Add a direction line and ovals for the eyes.

3. Connect the shapes and erase your guidelines. Add texture and other details.

# SATYR

This Greek mythological beast is half man and half horse.

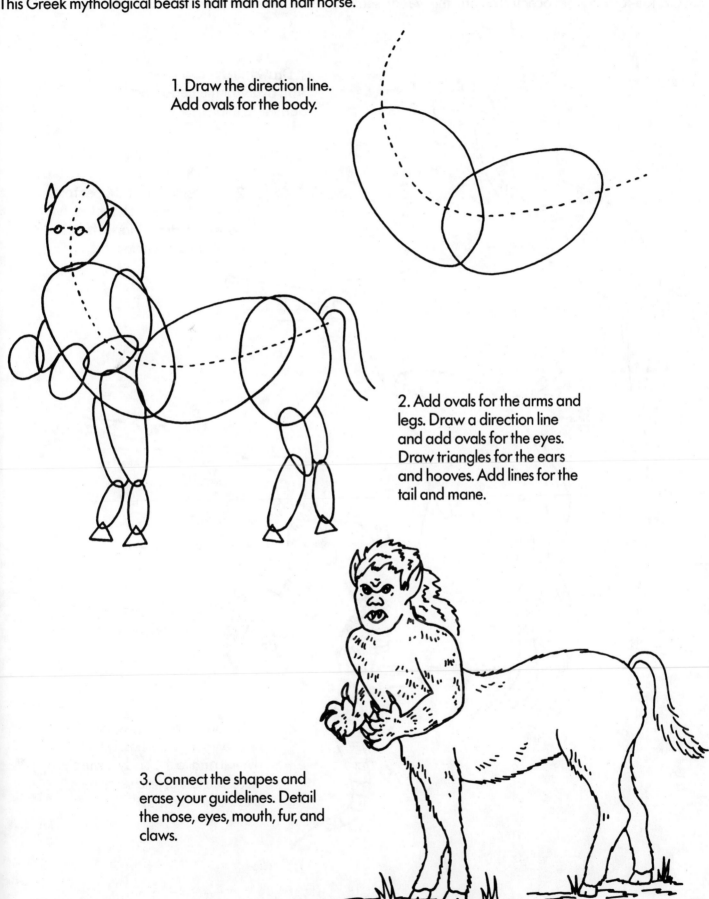

1. Draw the direction line. Add ovals for the body.

2. Add ovals for the arms and legs. Draw a direction line and add ovals for the eyes. Draw triangles for the ears and hooves. Add lines for the tail and mane.

3. Connect the shapes and erase your guidelines. Detail the nose, eyes, mouth, fur, and claws.

# WEEDY SEA DRAGON

A strange-looking real ocean creature, the weedy sea dragon looks a little like the dragons of myth.

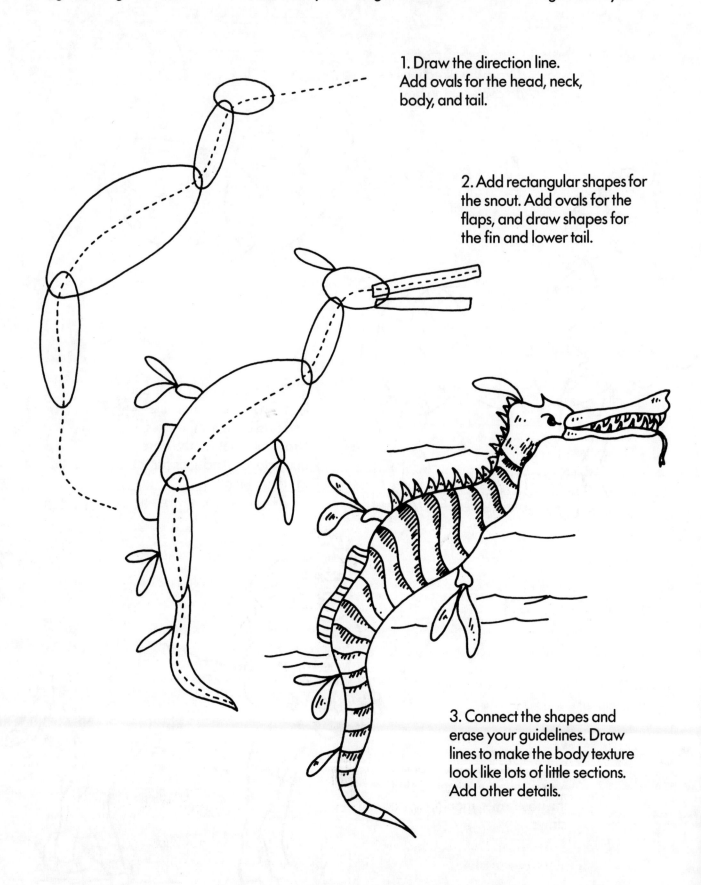

1. Draw the direction line. Add ovals for the head, neck, body, and tail.

2. Add rectangular shapes for the snout. Add ovals for the flaps, and draw shapes for the fin and lower tail.

3. Connect the shapes and erase your guidelines. Draw lines to make the body texture look like lots of little sections. Add other details.

# HAIRY BEAST

Many stories of monsters are based on big, strong, hairy apes.

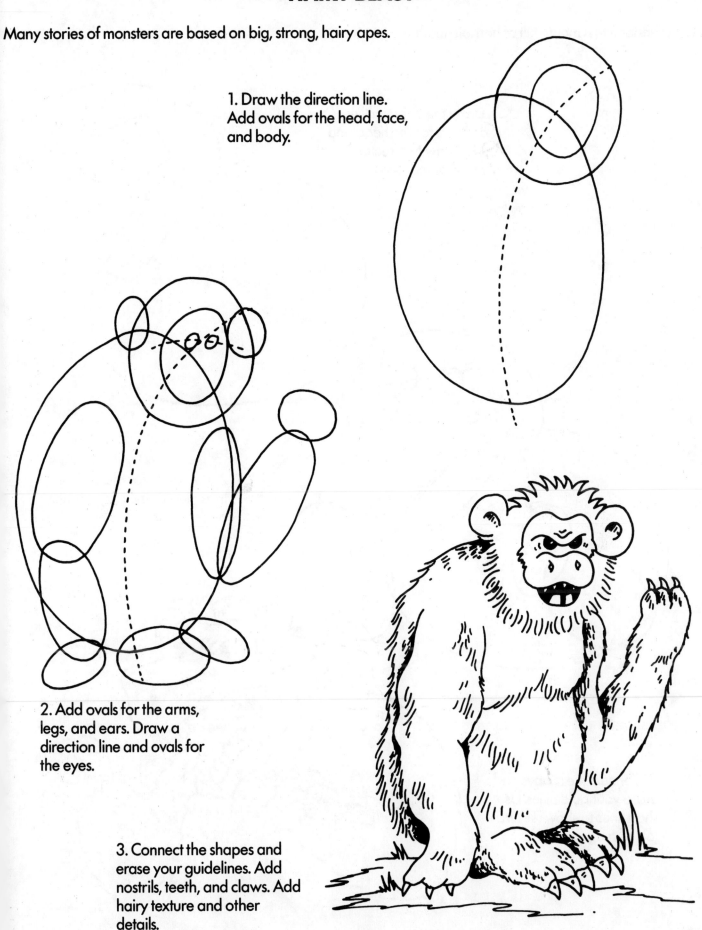

1. Draw the direction line. Add ovals for the head, face, and body.

2. Add ovals for the arms, legs, and ears. Draw a direction line and ovals for the eyes.

3. Connect the shapes and erase your guidelines. Add nostrils, teeth, and claws. Add hairy texture and other details.

15

# SNAGGLETOOTH

This monster has a mouth full of horrible teeth.

1. Draw the direction line. Add ovals for the head and body. Draw two rectangular shapes for the jaw.

2. Add ovals for the arms and triangles for the claws. Make ovals for the eyes.

3. Connect the shapes and erase your guidelines. Use short lines to show fur. Draw lots of snaggly teeth.

# SNAKE MONSTER

Here's a make-believe snake that turns into a monster!

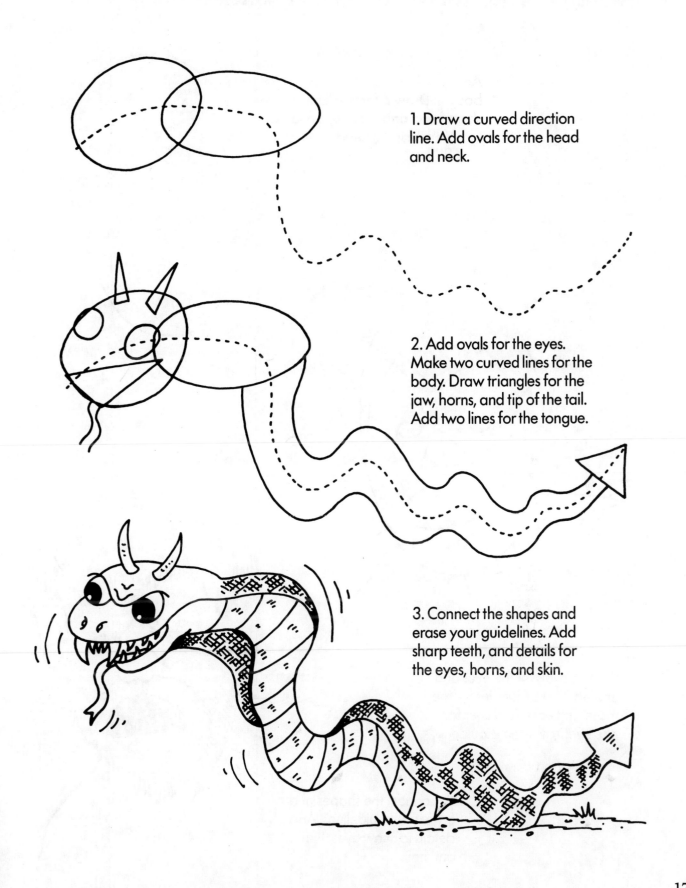

1. Draw a curved direction line. Add ovals for the head and neck.

2. Add ovals for the eyes. Make two curved lines for the body. Draw triangles for the jaw, horns, and tip of the tail. Add two lines for the tongue.

3. Connect the shapes and erase your guidelines. Add sharp teeth, and details for the eyes, horns, and skin.

# WEREWOLF

Werewolves are said to be humans who change into wolves during the full moon. According to folktales, they can be killed only by silver bullets. Let's start by drawing the werewolf's head.

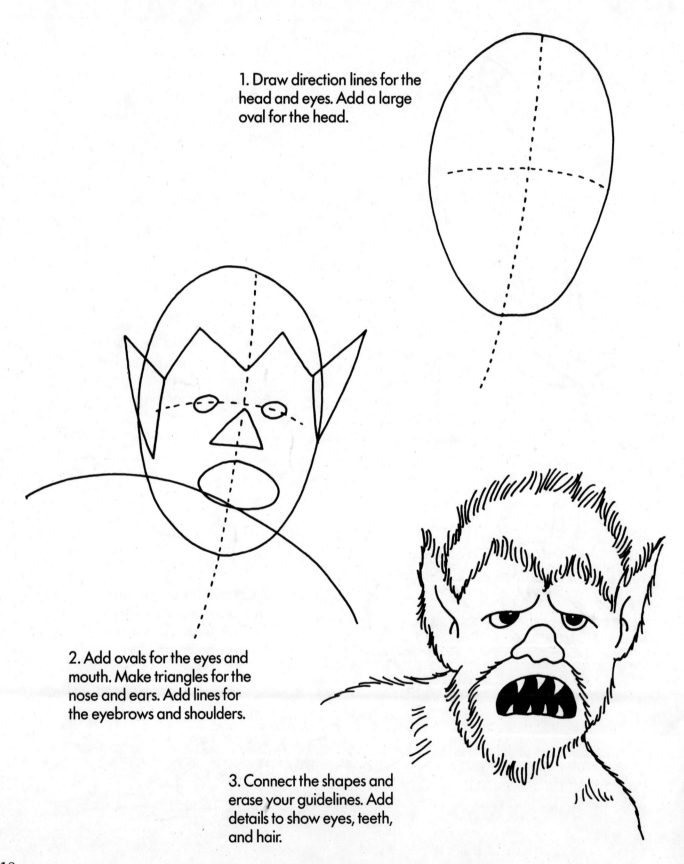

1. Draw direction lines for the head and eyes. Add a large oval for the head.

2. Add ovals for the eyes and mouth. Make triangles for the nose and ears. Add lines for the eyebrows and shoulders.

3. Connect the shapes and erase your guidelines. Add details to show eyes, teeth, and hair.

Now let's draw the werewolf's whole body.

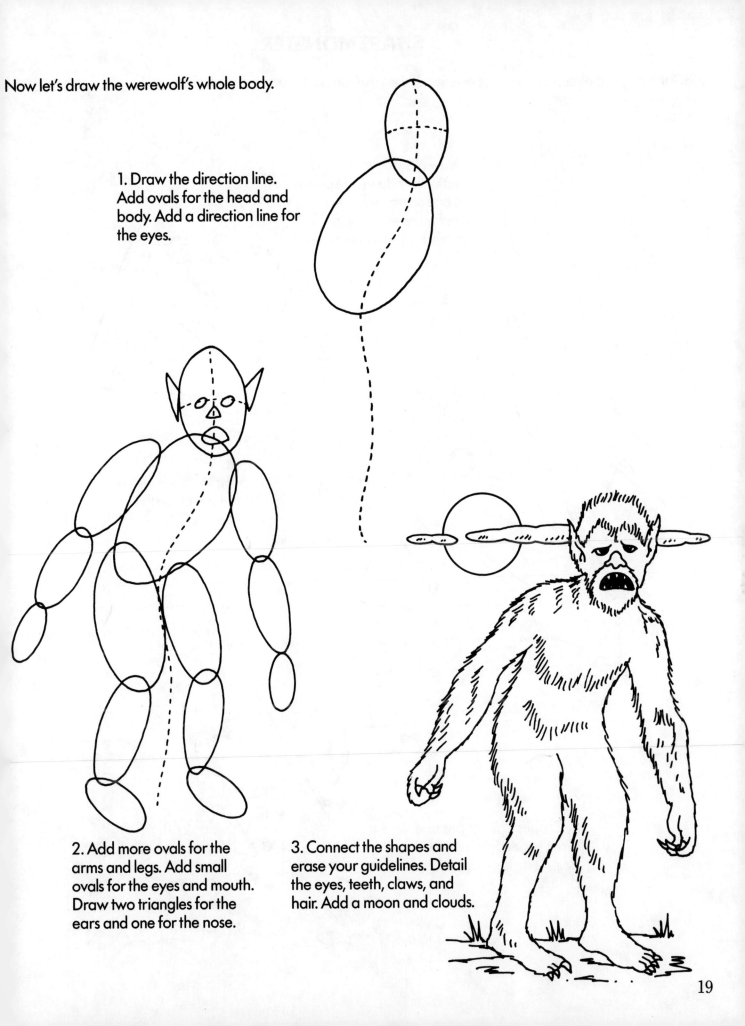

1. Draw the direction line. Add ovals for the head and body. Add a direction line for the eyes.

2. Add more ovals for the arms and legs. Add small ovals for the eyes and mouth. Draw two triangles for the ears and one for the nose.

3. Connect the shapes and erase your guidelines. Detail the eyes, teeth, claws, and hair. Add a moon and clouds.

19

# SHAPE MONSTER

Try making some monsters with geometric shapes for bodies. Here's one made from a triangle.

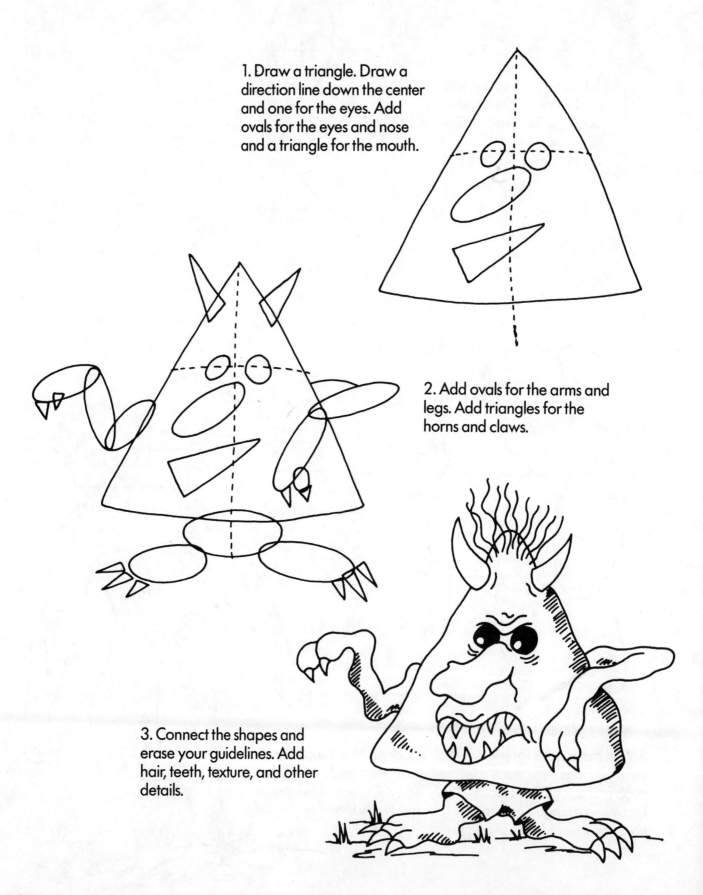

1. Draw a triangle. Draw a direction line down the center and one for the eyes. Add ovals for the eyes and nose and a triangle for the mouth.

2. Add ovals for the arms and legs. Add triangles for the horns and claws.

3. Connect the shapes and erase your guidelines. Add hair, teeth, texture, and other details.

# MONONGAHELA'S MONSTER

In 1852, whalers on the ship *Monongahela* killed a giant sea reptile 150 feet long. Unfortunately, on the trip home the ship sank, and no trace of it or the monster was ever found. Could this be the creature?

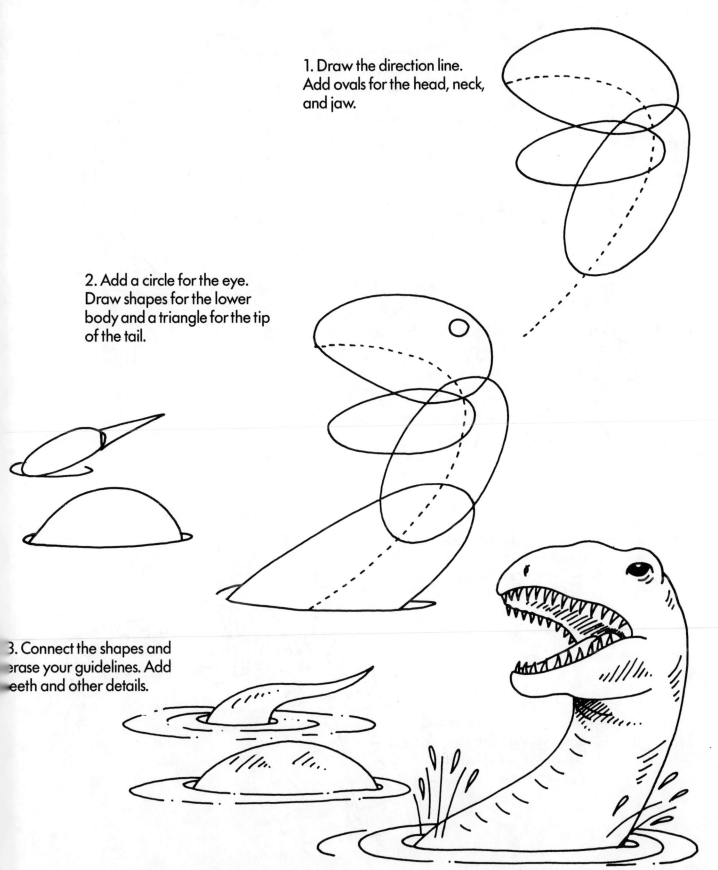

1. Draw the direction line. Add ovals for the head, neck, and jaw.

2. Add a circle for the eye. Draw shapes for the lower body and a triangle for the tip of the tail.

3. Connect the shapes and erase your guidelines. Add teeth and other details.

# MOVIE MONSTER

Many monsters in the movies are so big that they can destroy whole cities!

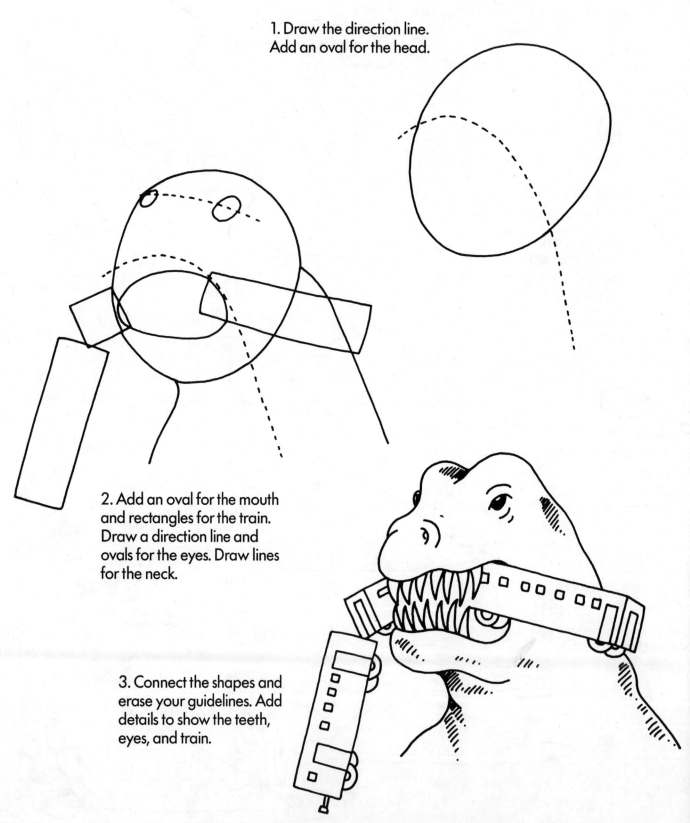

1. Draw the direction line.
Add an oval for the head.

2. Add an oval for the mouth
and rectangles for the train.
Draw a direction line and
ovals for the eyes. Draw lines
for the neck.

3. Connect the shapes and
erase your guidelines. Add
details to show the teeth,
eyes, and train.

# BIG EARS

This hairy monster has huge ears and sharp teeth!

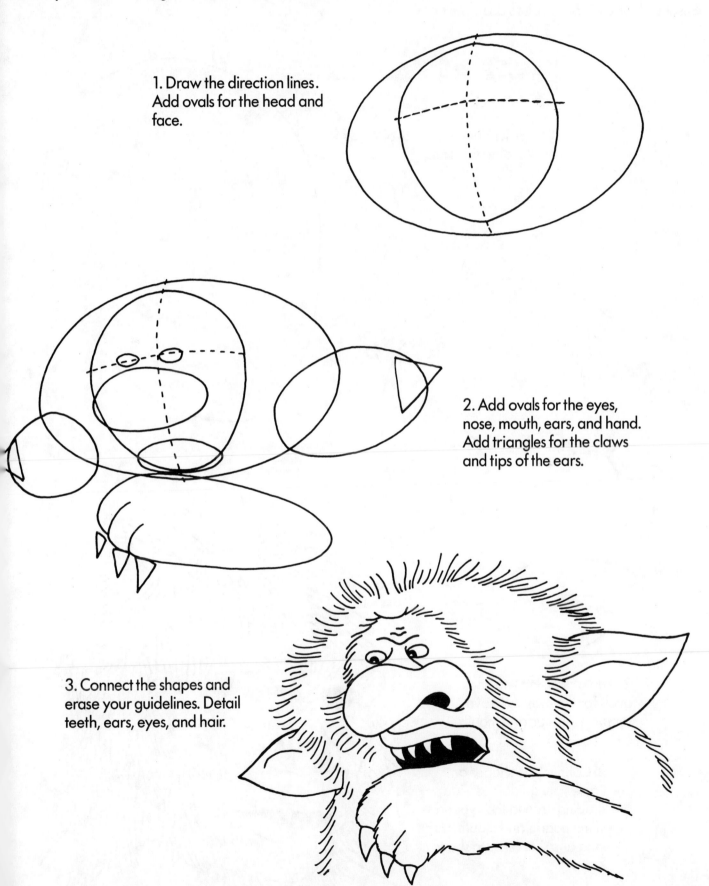

1. Draw the direction lines. Add ovals for the head and face.

2. Add ovals for the eyes, nose, mouth, ears, and hand. Add triangles for the claws and tips of the ears.

3. Connect the shapes and erase your guidelines. Detail teeth, ears, eyes, and hair.

# APE MAN

Many stories have been told about a huge ape man. In Asia it is called Yeti. In North America it is called Sasquatch or Bigfoot. First, let's draw the head.

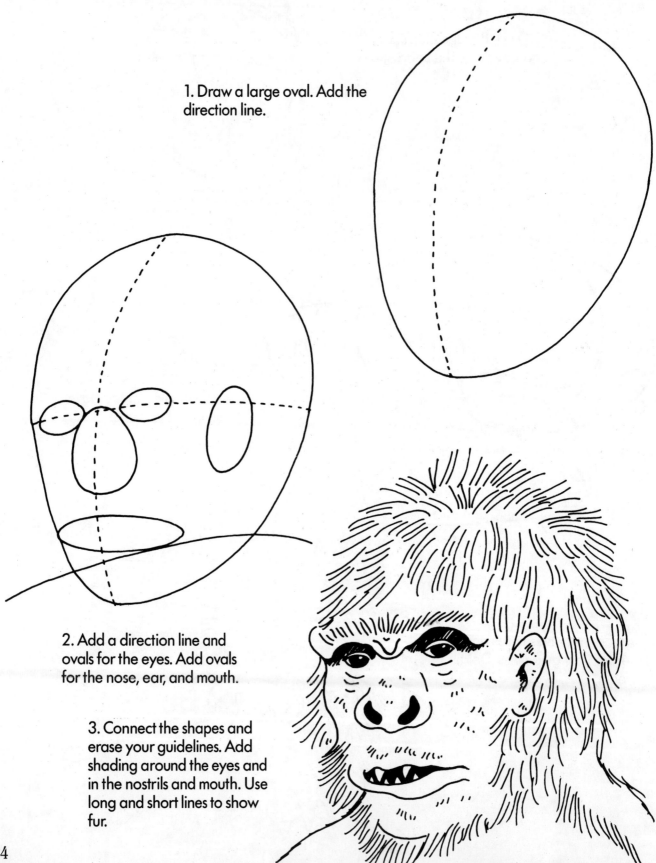

1. Draw a large oval. Add the direction line.

2. Add a direction line and ovals for the eyes. Add ovals for the nose, ear, and mouth.

3. Connect the shapes and erase your guidelines. Add shading around the eyes and in the nostrils and mouth. Use long and short lines to show fur.

Now let's draw the ape man's full body.

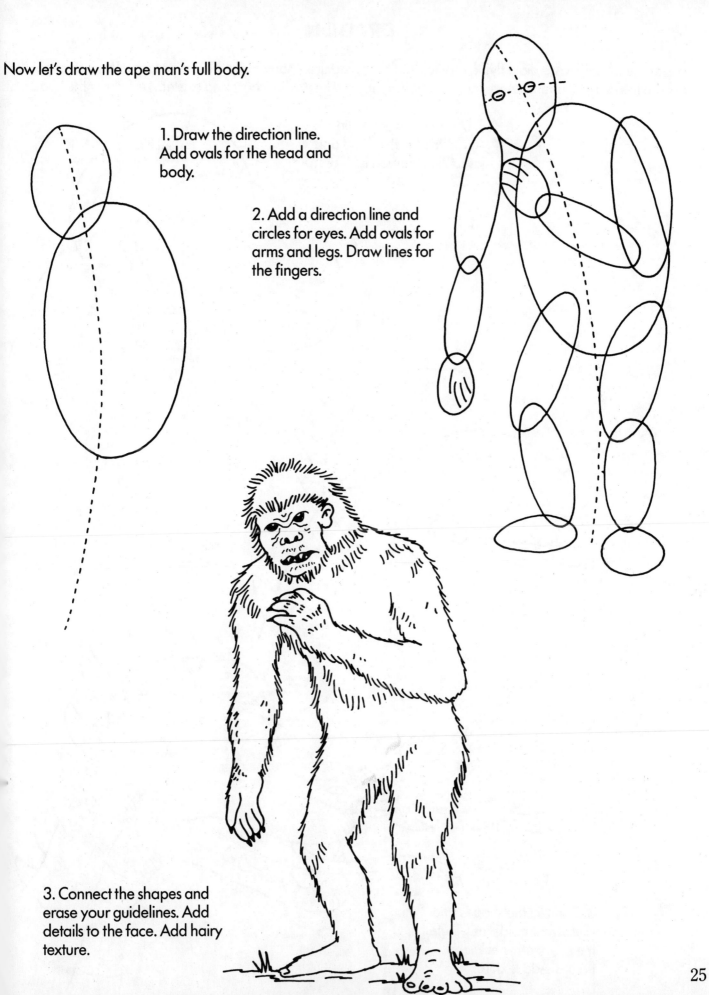

1. Draw the direction line. Add ovals for the head and body.

2. Add a direction line and circles for eyes. Add ovals for arms and legs. Draw lines for the fingers.

3. Connect the shapes and erase your guidelines. Add details to the face. Add hairy texture.

# DRAGON

Dragons were said to be giant flying reptiles that breathed fire. Many looked like dinosaurs. This is strange because the dragon legends were told long before anyone knew dinosaurs had existed. Let's draw the head first.

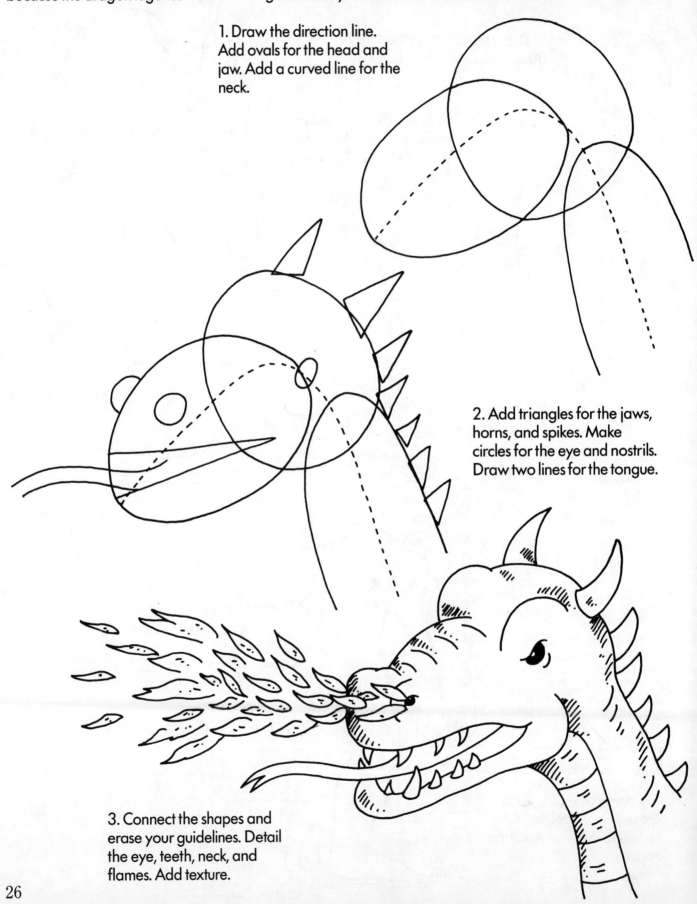

1. Draw the direction line. Add ovals for the head and jaw. Add a curved line for the neck.

2. Add triangles for the jaws, horns, and spikes. Make circles for the eye and nostrils. Draw two lines for the tongue.

3. Connect the shapes and erase your guidelines. Detail the eye, teeth, neck, and flames. Add texture.

Now let's draw the whole dragon.

1. Draw the direction line. Add ovals for the head, neck, and body.

2. Add ovals for the legs. Draw shapes for the wings and tail. Add a triangle for the tip of the tail.

3. Connect the shapes and erase your guidelines. Add details to show teeth, claws, horns, tongue, eye, and flames.

# GREAT WHITE SHARK

The great white shark's powerful jaws, filled with sharp teeth, can crush a small boat. The average great white shark can be up to 18 feet long.

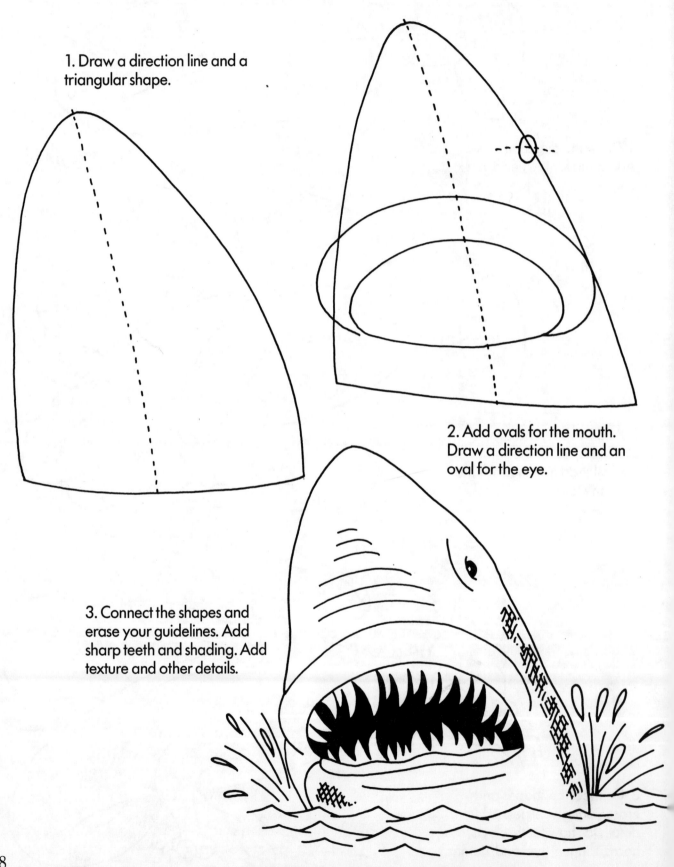

1. Draw a direction line and a triangular shape.

2. Add ovals for the mouth. Draw a direction line and an oval for the eye.

3. Connect the shapes and erase your guidelines. Add sharp teeth and shading. Add texture and other details.

# DEVIL

Devils are evil spirits who are said to live in Hell. Their favorite sport is trying to get people to do bad things.

1. Draw the direction line. Add an egg shape for the head and a triangle for the beard.

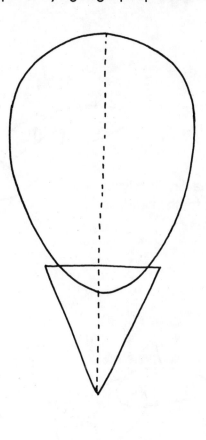

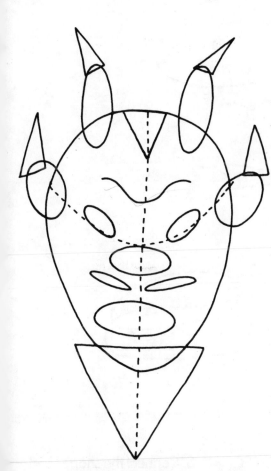

2. Add a direction line and ovals for the eyes. Draw ovals for the nose, mustache, and mouth. Add a line for the wrinkle in the forehead. Make circles and triangles for the horns and ears. Add another triangle for the hair at the top of the head.

3. Connect the shapes and erase your guidelines. Fill in the mustache, beard, and hair. Add texture and other details.

29

# WINGED MONSTER

Here's a monster based on the Komodo Dragon, a giant creature that lived on the island of Komodo and ate pigs and goats.

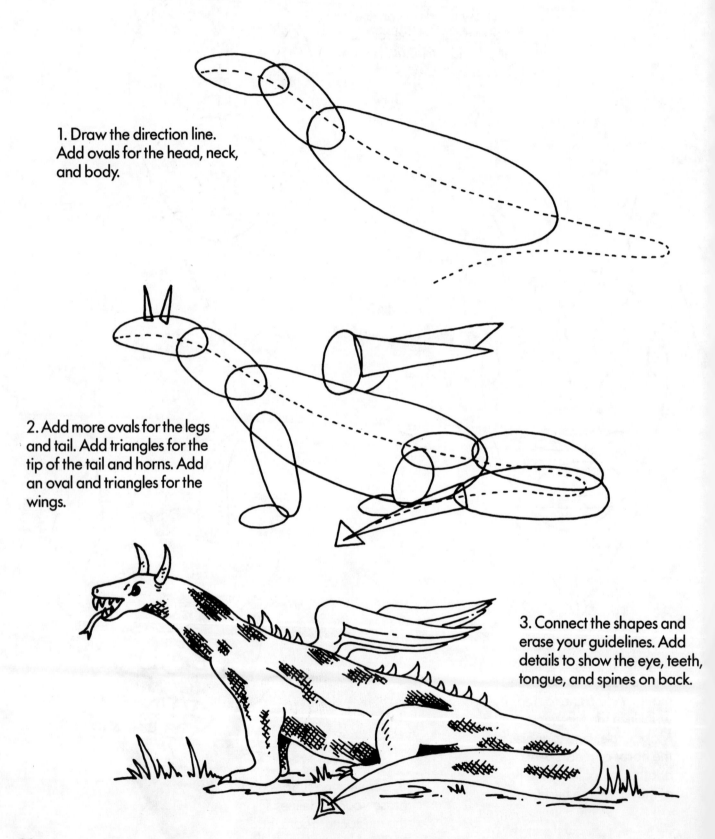

1. Draw the direction line. Add ovals for the head, neck, and body.

2. Add more ovals for the legs and tail. Add triangles for the tip of the tail and horns. Add an oval and triangles for the wings.

3. Connect the shapes and erase your guidelines. Add details to show the eye, teeth, tongue, and spines on back.

# WITCH

Witches are supposed to possess magic powers. They are usually shown with pointed hats.

1. Draw the direction line. Add ovals for the head, neck, nose, and chin.

2. Add ovals and a triangle for the hat. Draw ovals for the eyes and a triangle for the mouth. Add lines for the shoulders.

3. Connect the shapes and erase your guidelines. Detail the hair, teeth, and eyes.

31

# CLAWS

This monster seems to be all claws!

1. Draw the direction line. Add ovals for the head, neck, and body.

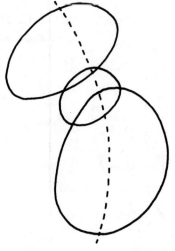

2. Add an oval for the hair. Add triangles for the horns. Draw a direction line and ovals for the eyes. Add ovals for the arms and legs. Make triangles for the claws.

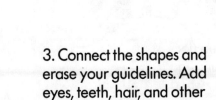

3. Connect the shapes and erase your guidelines. Add eyes, teeth, hair, and other details.

# MUMMY

Ancient Egyptians wrapped dead bodies for burial. In movies and stories these mummies roam around, scaring everyone.

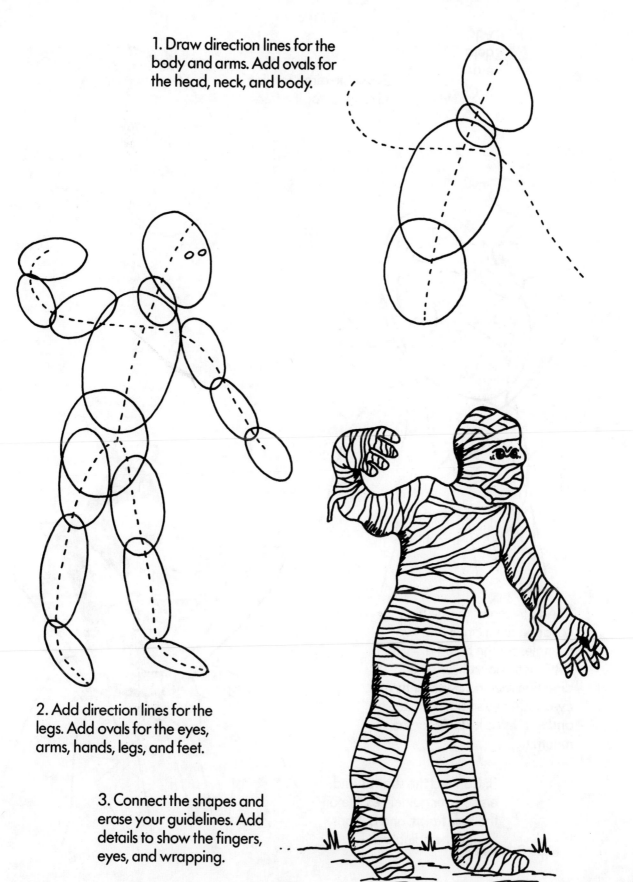

1. Draw direction lines for the body and arms. Add ovals for the head, neck, and body.

2. Add direction lines for the legs. Add ovals for the eyes, arms, hands, legs, and feet.

3. Connect the shapes and erase your guidelines. Add details to show the fingers, eyes, and wrapping.

# VAMPIRE

Vampires are said to suck the blood of living creatures. They fly by night and must return to their coffins before daybreak, or the sun will destroy them!

1. Draw the direction line. Add an oval for the head.

2. Add triangles for the high collar. Make a circle and two triangles for the bow tie. Add lines for the jacket. Draw a direction line and ovals for the eyes. Add ovals for the nose and ear and a triangle for the mouth.

3. Connect the shapes and erase your guidelines. Detail the hair, fangs, and buttons. Shade the hair black.

# BIG NOSE

This monster's biggest feature is its nose!

1. Draw the direction line. Add ovals for the head, body, arms, and legs.

2. Draw another direction line and ovals for the eyes. Add ovals for the ears and rectangles for the jaws and nose. Add triangles for the claws, tip of the tail, and tips of the ears.

3. Connect the shapes and erase your guidelines. Draw eyes and sharp teeth. Add texture and other details.

# TROLL

Trolls are little elves with huge noses, long tails, and claws.

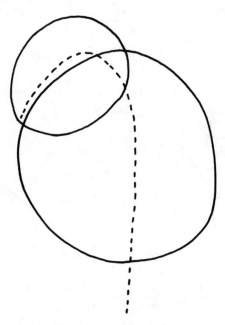

1. Draw the direction line. Add ovals for the head and body.

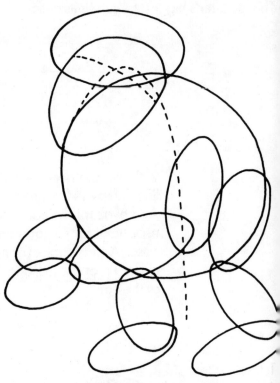

2. Add ovals for the arms, legs, and top of the head. Draw a direction line for the eyes.

3. Draw ovals for the eyes, nose, and ears. Add two lines and an oval for the tail.

4. Connect the shapes and erase your guidelines. Detail the eyes, teeth, claws, and fur.

# CYCLOPS

Cyclops was a giant in Greek myth. It had one eye in the center of its forehead. In the story of Odysseus, a Cyclops ate some of Odysseus' men and captured the rest. Odysseus blinded the sleeping giant with a red-hot stake.  Let's draw the Cyclops's head first.

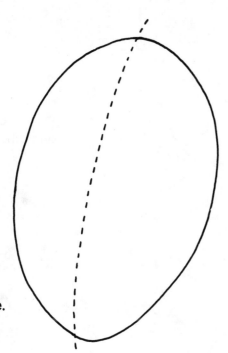

1. Draw the direction line. Add a large oval for the head.

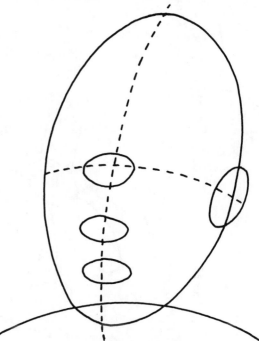

2. Add a direction line and oval for the eye. Add ovals for the nose, mouth, and ear. Draw a line for the shoulders.

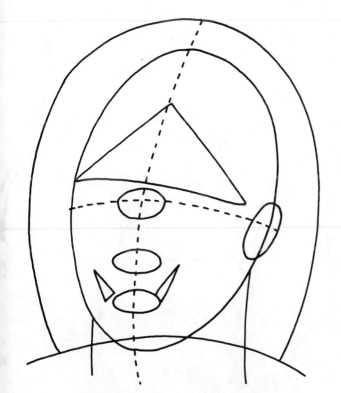

3. Make two triangles for the fangs and one on the forehead. Add a shape for the outside edge of the hair and two lines for the neck.

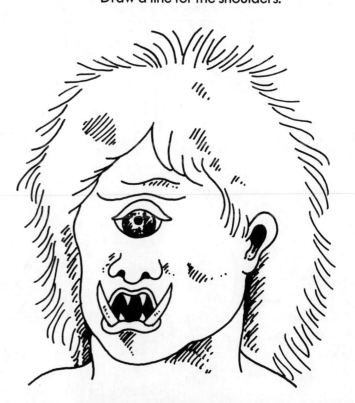

4. Connect the shapes and erase your guidelines. Add texture and other details.

Now let's draw Cyclops's full body.

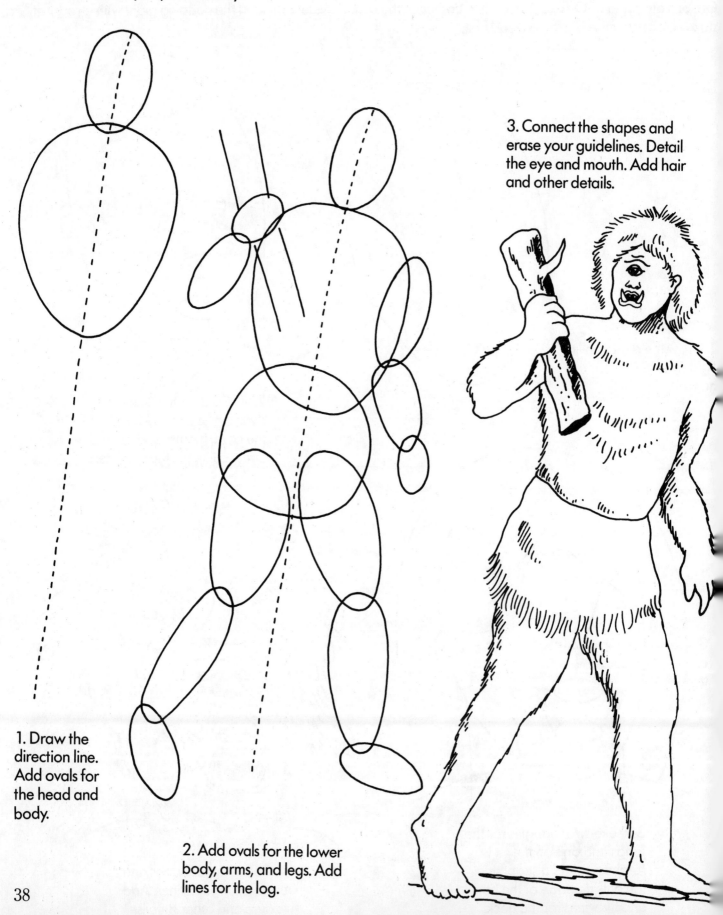

3. Connect the shapes and erase your guidelines. Detail the eye and mouth. Add hair and other details.

1. Draw the direction line. Add ovals for the head and body.

2. Add ovals for the lower body, arms, and legs. Add lines for the log.

# BASILISK LIZARD

Movie makers often use small lizards like this one and make them appear huge on screen. Enlarged, these modern lizards are fierce looking.

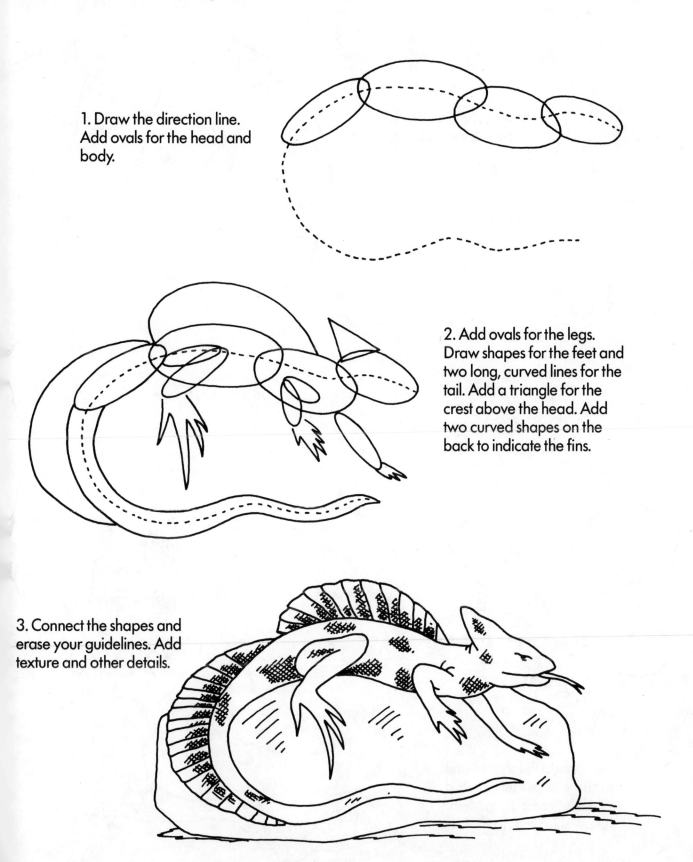

1. Draw the direction line. Add ovals for the head and body.

2. Add ovals for the legs. Draw shapes for the feet and two long, curved lines for the tail. Add a triangle for the crest above the head. Add two curved shapes on the back to indicate the fins.

3. Connect the shapes and erase your guidelines. Add texture and other details.

# TWO-HORNED MONSTER

This monster has big horns, sharp teeth, and spiky hair.

1. Draw the direction line. Add ovals for the body, head, and jaw.

2. Add ovals for the legs, eyes, and arm. Add triangles for the horns and claws.

3. Connect the shapes and erase your guidelines. Add spiky hair and sharp teeth. Draw short lines to show fur.

# BAT

Most bats are harmless, but they look scary. This is a fruit-eating bat. First let's draw the bat's head.

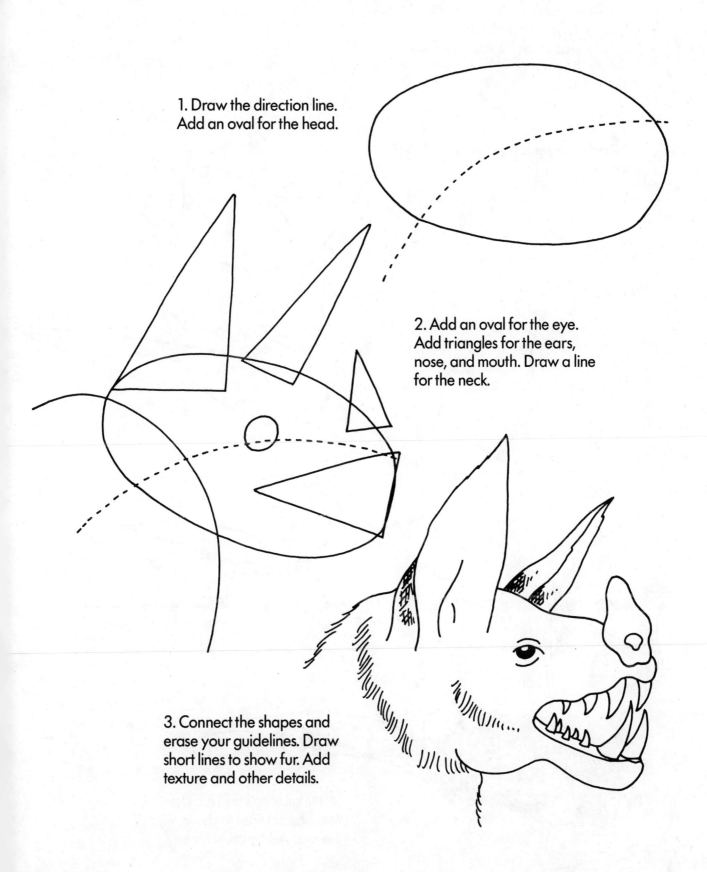

1. Draw the direction line. Add an oval for the head.

2. Add an oval for the eye. Add triangles for the ears, nose, and mouth. Draw a line for the neck.

3. Connect the shapes and erase your guidelines. Draw short lines to show fur. Add texture and other details.

Now let's draw the bat's full body.

1. Draw the direction line. Add ovals for the head and body.

2. Add triangles for the wings and ears.

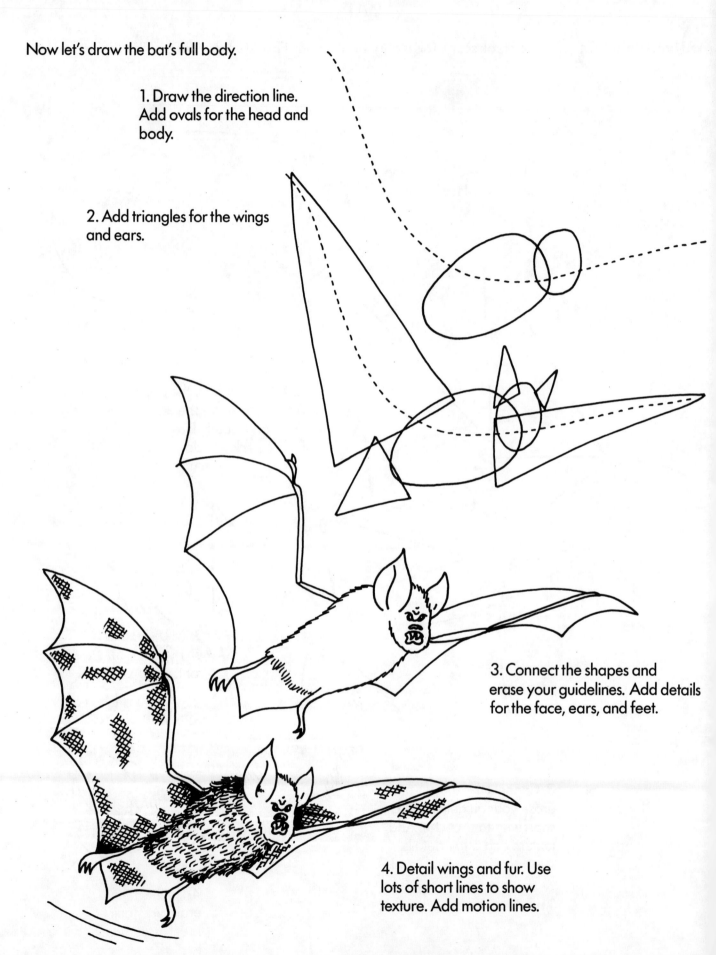

3. Connect the shapes and erase your guidelines. Add details for the face, ears, and feet.

4. Detail wings and fur. Use lots of short lines to show texture. Add motion lines.

# GATOR MONSTER

An alligator makes a good basis for a monster. This one has spikes on its back and lots of sharp teeth.

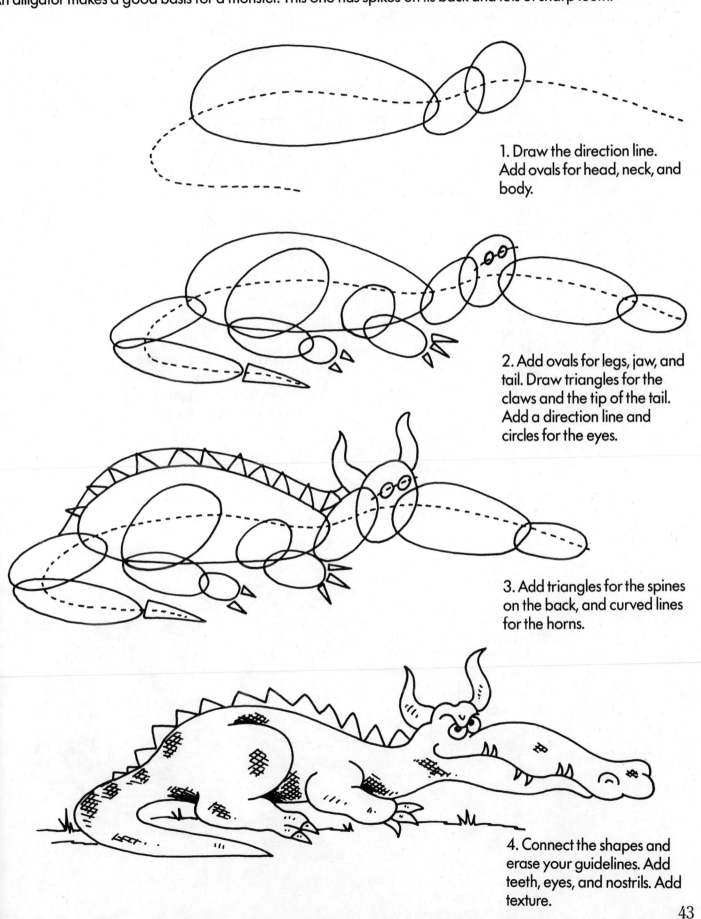

1. Draw the direction line. Add ovals for head, neck, and body.

2. Add ovals for legs, jaw, and tail. Draw triangles for the claws and the tip of the tail. Add a direction line and circles for the eyes.

3. Add triangles for the spines on the back, and curved lines for the horns.

4. Connect the shapes and erase your guidelines. Add teeth, eyes, and nostrils. Add texture.

# SPHINX

The Sphinx was a monster of Greek myth with the head of a woman and the body of a lion. She asked riddles of everyone. If they could not answer them, she killed them.

1. Draw the direction line. Add ovals for the head, neck, and body.

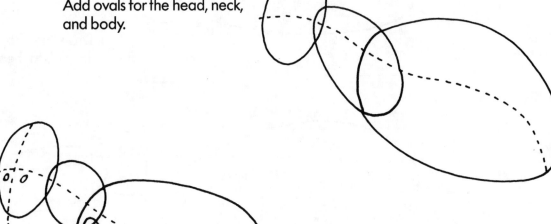

2. Draw the direction line and ovals for the eyes. Add ovals for the legs. Add lines and an oval for the tail.

3. Connect the shapes and erase your guidelines. Use short lines to show fur and long lines for the woman's hair. Add details to the face, fingers, and claws.

# SQUIGGLY MONSTER

Many stories have been told about a giant octopus that terrorizes seamen and sinks ships.

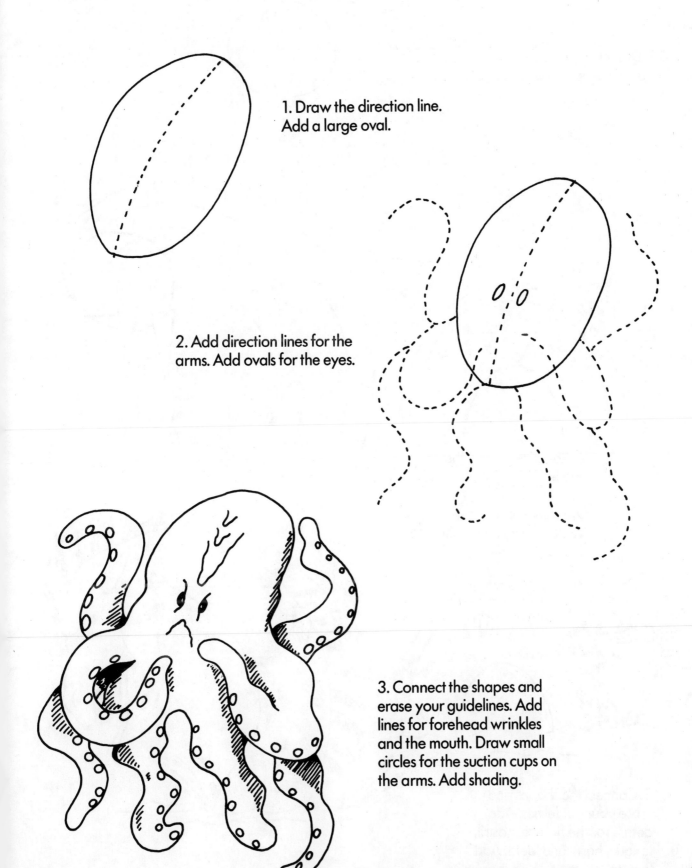

1. Draw the direction line. Add a large oval.

2. Add direction lines for the arms. Add ovals for the eyes.

3. Connect the shapes and erase your guidelines. Add lines for forehead wrinkles and the mouth. Draw small circles for the suction cups on the arms. Add shading.

# SEA MONSTER

In Greek myth, the sea god Neptune sent sea monsters to destroy people with whom he was angry.

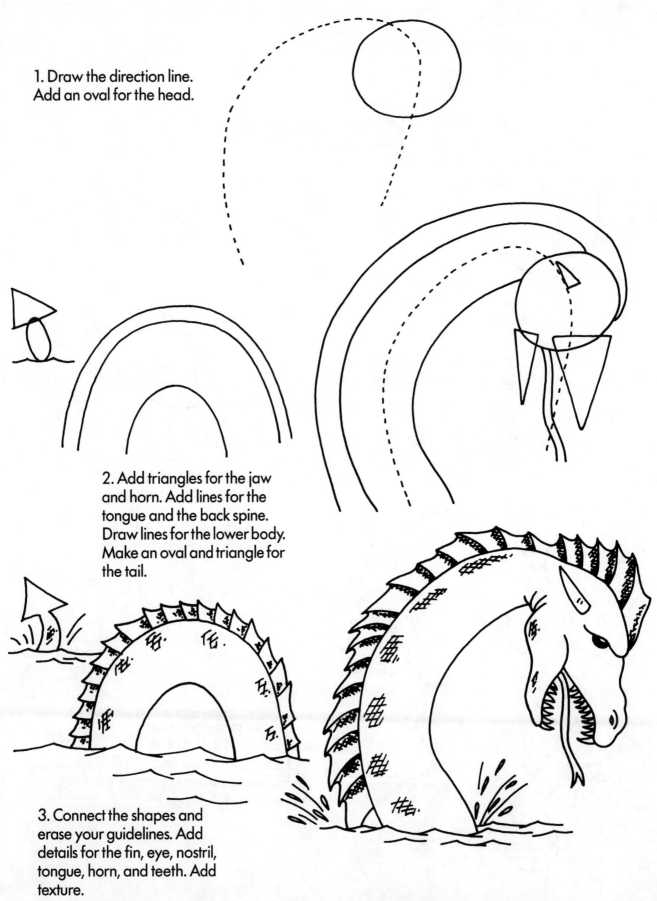

1. Draw the direction line. Add an oval for the head.

2. Add triangles for the jaw and horn. Add lines for the tongue and the back spine. Draw lines for the lower body. Make an oval and triangle for the tail.

3. Connect the shapes and erase your guidelines. Add details for the fin, eye, nostril, tongue, horn, and teeth. Add texture.

46

# EVIL GNOME

Beware of the evil gnome if you walk into a dark forest! Let's draw the gnome's head first.

1. Draw the direction line. Add an oval for the head.

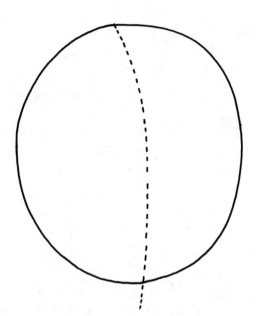

2. Draw the direction line and ovals for the eyes. Add ovals for the mouth and ears. Add triangles for the horns and nose. Draw two lines for the shoulders.

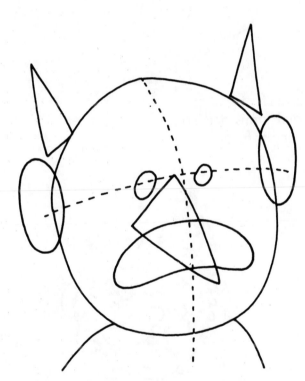

3. Connect the shapes and erase your guidelines. Detail the eyes, teeth, and hair. Add wrinkles on the forehead and chin and under the eyes. Add texture and shadow.

Now let's draw the gnome's full body.

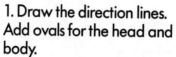

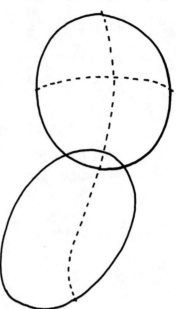

1. Draw the direction lines. Add ovals for the head and body.

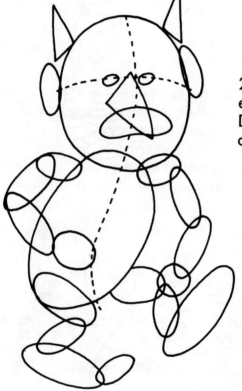

2. Add ovals for the ears, eyes, mouth, arms, and legs. Draw triangles for the horns and nose.

3. Connect the shapes and erase your guidelines. Add details for the hair and teeth. Add texture and other details.

48

# EVIL EYE

Here's a monster with an almost-human but scary face.

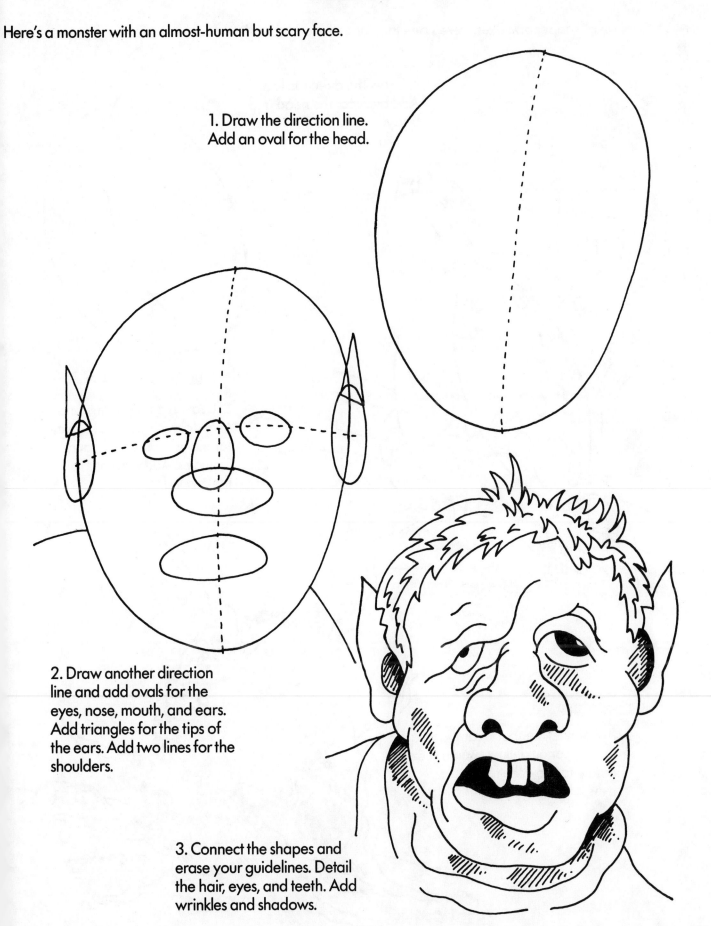

1. Draw the direction line. Add an oval for the head.

2. Draw another direction line and add ovals for the eyes, nose, mouth, and ears. Add triangles for the tips of the ears. Add two lines for the shoulders.

3. Connect the shapes and erase your guidelines. Detail the hair, eyes, and teeth. Add wrinkles and shadows.

49

# ALIEN

Aliens come in all shapes and sizes. Here's one that looks like a blob with tentacles.

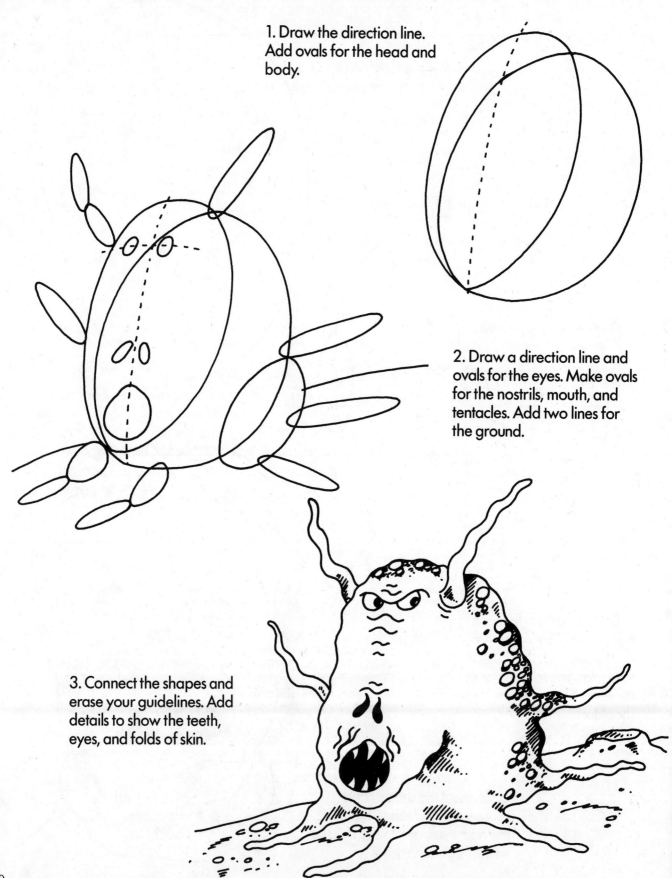

1. Draw the direction line. Add ovals for the head and body.

2. Draw a direction line and ovals for the eyes. Make ovals for the nostrils, mouth, and tentacles. Add two lines for the ground.

3. Connect the shapes and erase your guidelines. Add details to show the teeth, eyes, and folds of skin.

# FLYING BEAST

Here's a flying beast with an alligator's head, a snake's tongue, a bat's wings, and a dragon's tail.

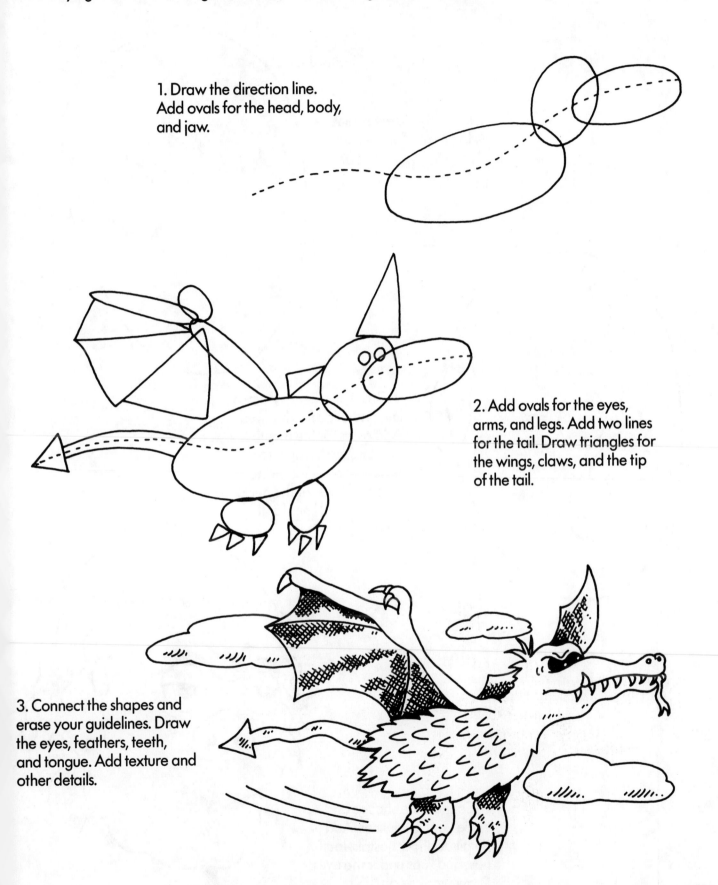

1. Draw the direction line. Add ovals for the head, body, and jaw.

2. Add ovals for the eyes, arms, and legs. Add two lines for the tail. Draw triangles for the wings, claws, and the tip of the tail.

3. Connect the shapes and erase your guidelines. Draw the eyes, feathers, teeth, and tongue. Add texture and other details.

# ZOMBIE

It is said that a zombie is a dead person who rises from the grave and roams at night.

1. Draw the direction line. Add an oval for the head.

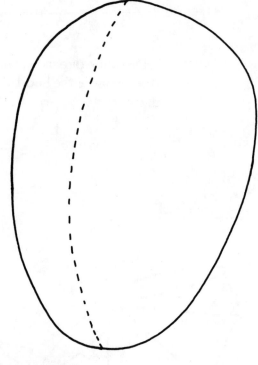

2. Draw another direction line and ovals for the eyes. Add ovals for the mouth and ear. Make a triangle for the nose and ovals for the nostrils. Add two lines for the neck. Draw curved lines for the mouth.

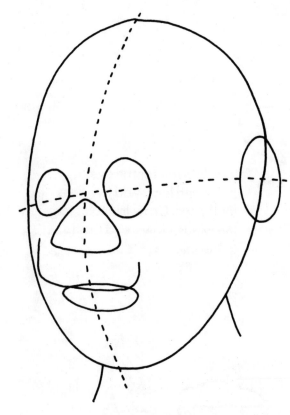

3. Connect the shapes and erase your guidelines. Add details to show nostrils, teeth, hair, and lines under the eyes. Draw wrinkles on the forehead.

# TREE MONSTER

You can make a monster out of almost anything. Here's a tree that's become a monster with scary eyes and fangs.

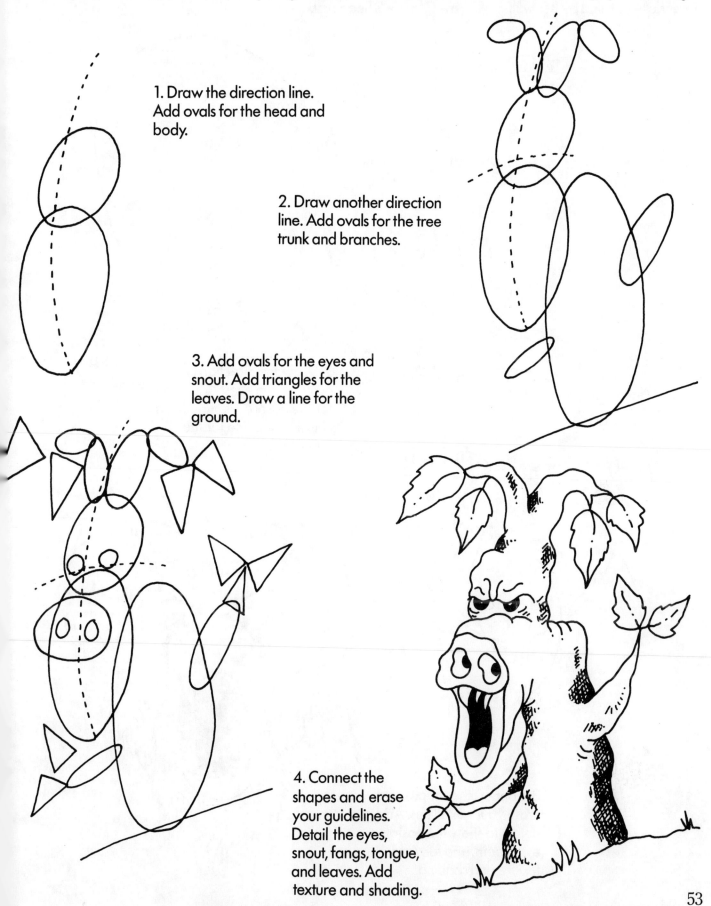

1. Draw the direction line. Add ovals for the head and body.

2. Draw another direction line. Add ovals for the tree trunk and branches.

3. Add ovals for the eyes and snout. Add triangles for the leaves. Draw a line for the ground.

4. Connect the shapes and erase your guidelines. Detail the eyes, snout, fangs, tongue, and leaves. Add texture and shading.

53

# GRENDEL

Grendel was a monster who lived in the marshes in Denmark over 1200 years ago. He liked to eat people. Grendel was killed by Beowulf. Let's draw Grendel's head first.

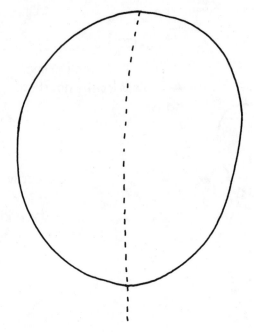

1. Draw the direction line. Add an oval for the head.

2. Draw the direction line and ovals for the eyes. Add ovals for the nose, ears, mouth, and chin. Draw a line for the shoulders.

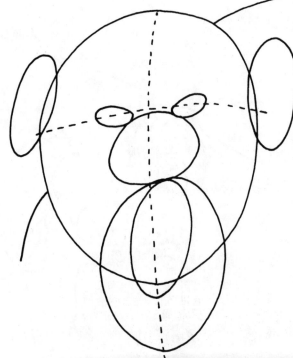

3. Connect the shapes and erase your guidelines. Add details to show the nostrils, eyes, teeth, and fur. Add texture and shading.

**Now let's draw Grendel's full body.**

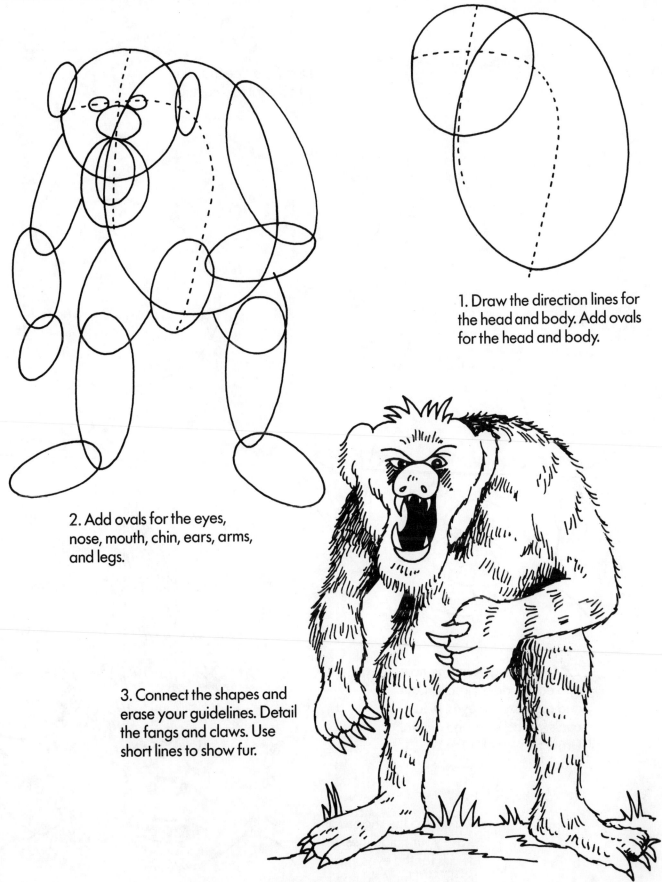

1. Draw the direction lines for the head and body. Add ovals for the head and body.

2. Add ovals for the eyes, nose, mouth, chin, ears, arms, and legs.

3. Connect the shapes and erase your guidelines. Detail the fangs and claws. Use short lines to show fur.

# GOBLIN

Goblins are evil spirits that are full of mischief. They look like little men dressed in black with furry pointed heads.

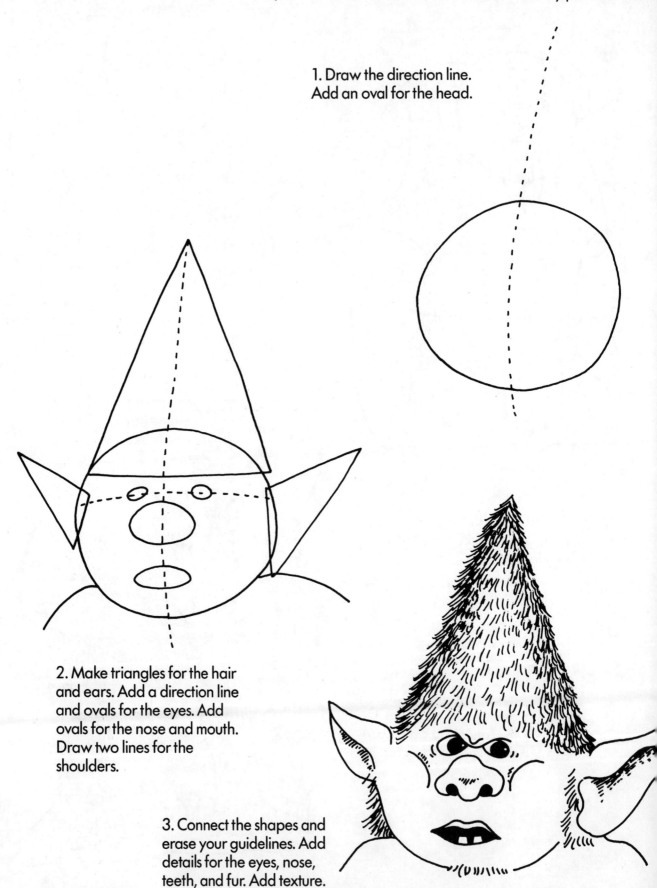

1. Draw the direction line. Add an oval for the head.

2. Make triangles for the hair and ears. Add a direction line and ovals for the eyes. Add ovals for the nose and mouth. Draw two lines for the shoulders.

3. Connect the shapes and erase your guidelines. Add details for the eyes, nose, teeth, and fur. Add texture.

# FRIZZLETOP

Here's a monster with lots of frizzy hair, and a horn on its nose!

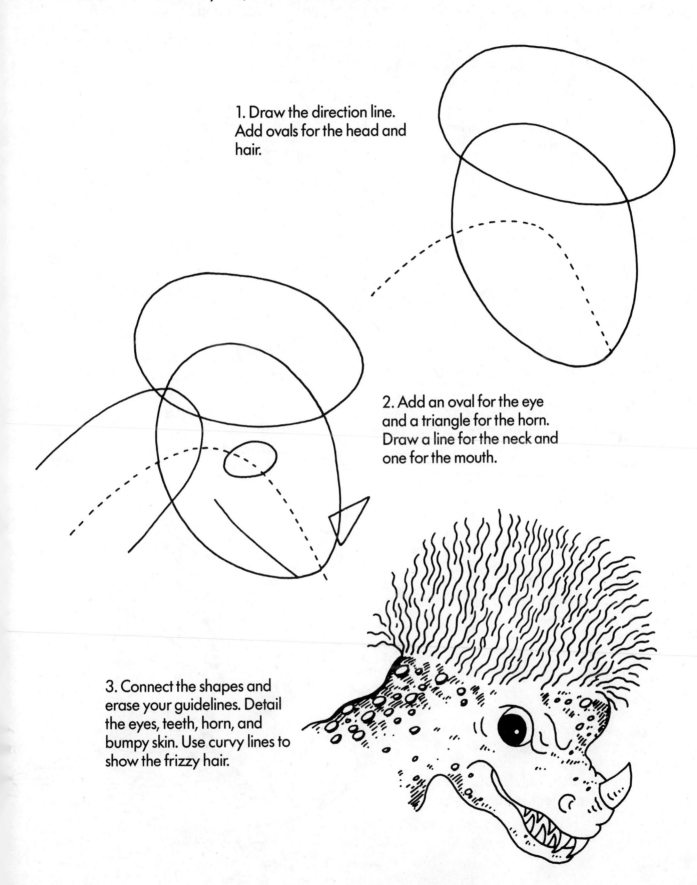

1. Draw the direction line. Add ovals for the head and hair.

2. Add an oval for the eye and a triangle for the horn. Draw a line for the neck and one for the mouth.

3. Connect the shapes and erase your guidelines. Detail the eyes, teeth, horn, and bumpy skin. Use curvy lines to show the frizzy hair.

# SIRENS

In Greek myth, sirens had the heads of beautiful women and the bodies of birds. They sang songs so lovely that no man could resist them. Sailors would dive into the sea to find the sirens — and drown.

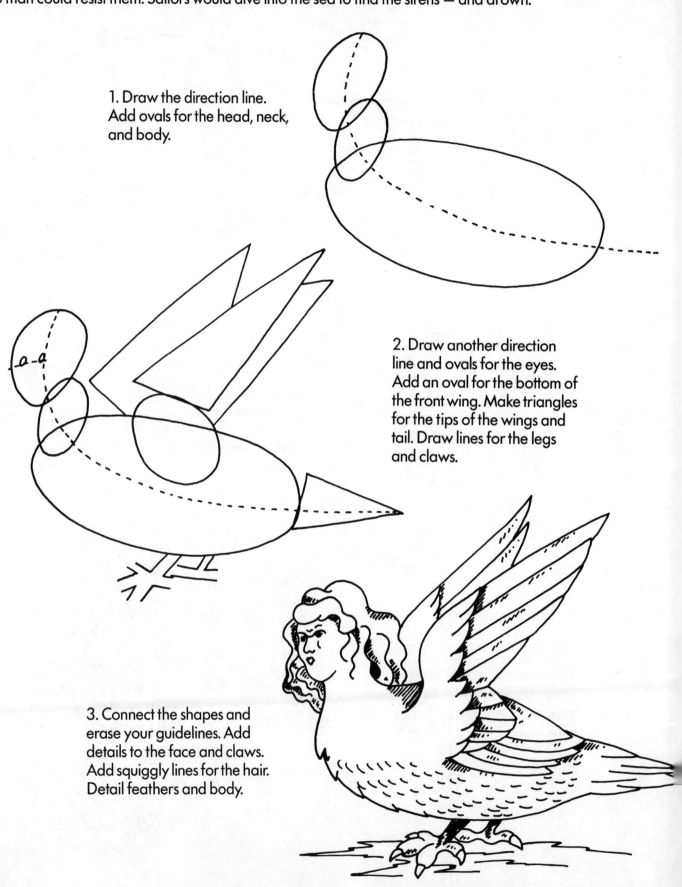

1. Draw the direction line. Add ovals for the head, neck, and body.

2. Draw another direction line and ovals for the eyes. Add an oval for the bottom of the front wing. Make triangles for the tips of the wings and tail. Draw lines for the legs and claws.

3. Connect the shapes and erase your guidelines. Add details to the face and claws. Add squiggly lines for the hair. Detail feathers and body.

# GRIFFIN

In ancient myths of the Middle East, the griffin had the head, wings, and claws of an eagle and the body of a lion. It was as strong as 100 eagles.

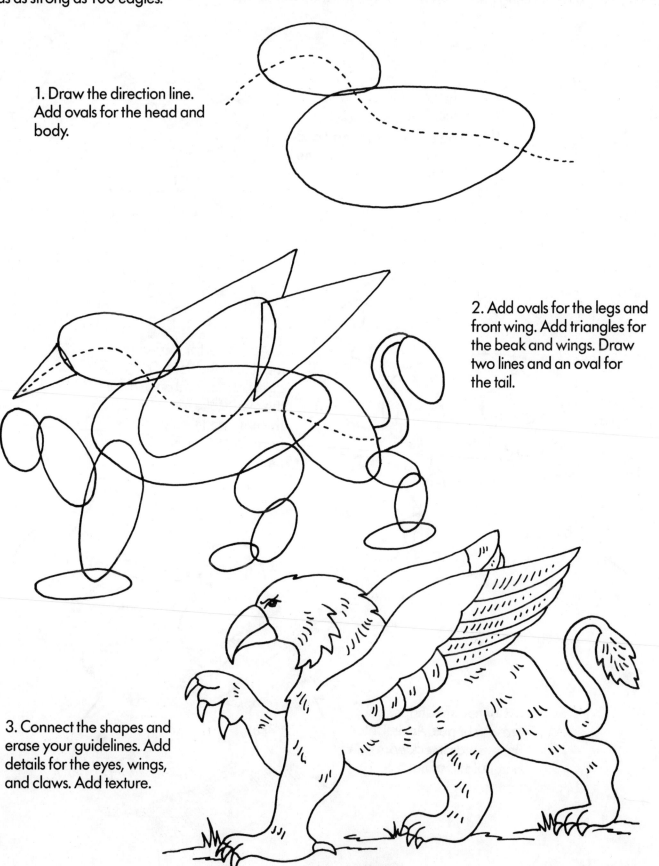

1. Draw the direction line. Add ovals for the head and body.

2. Add ovals for the legs and front wing. Add triangles for the beak and wings. Draw two lines and an oval for the tail.

3. Connect the shapes and erase your guidelines. Add details for the eyes, wings, and claws. Add texture.

59

# MINOTAUR

In Greek myth, the Minotaur was part bull and part man. It lived on the island of Crete inside a large maze. Every year the king sent 14 young people into the maze, and they were eaten by the monster. Let's draw the head first.

1. Draw the direction line. Add ovals for the head and horns and a triangle for the jaw.

2. Add ovals for the ear and the ring in the nose. Draw a direction line and an oval for the eye. Make triangles for the nose and the tips of the horns. Add two lines for the neck.

3. Connect the shapes and erase your guidelines. Detail the eye, hair, teeth, horns, and ring. Add shading.

Now let's draw the Minotaur's full body.

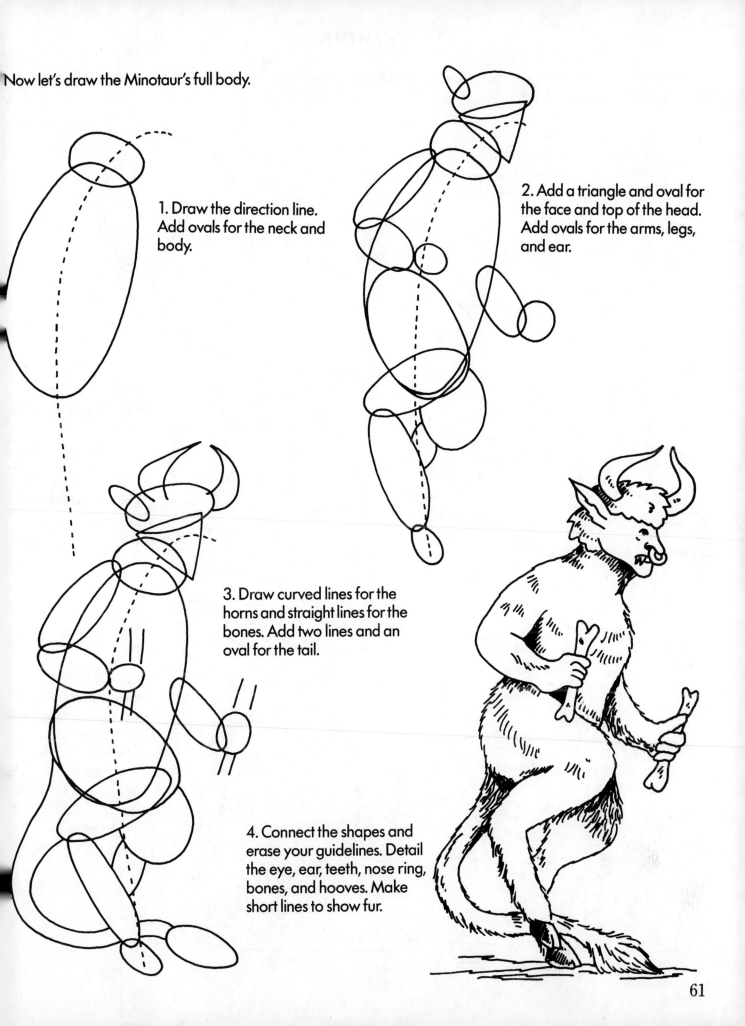

1. Draw the direction line. Add ovals for the neck and body.

2. Add a triangle and oval for the face and top of the head. Add ovals for the arms, legs, and ear.

3. Draw curved lines for the horns and straight lines for the bones. Add two lines and an oval for the tail.

4. Connect the shapes and erase your guidelines. Detail the eye, ear, teeth, nose ring, bones, and hooves. Make short lines to show fur.

# CHIMERA

The Chimera was one of the strangest-looking creatures in Greek myth. It was a combination of a lion, a goat, and a snake that breathed fire.

1. Draw the direction line. Add ovals for the heads and body.

2. Add ovals for the legs. Draw two lines and an oval for the snake-tail. Add triangles for the claws and lion's nose. Draw a direction line and ovals for the lion's eyes. Draw curved lines for the lion's mouth and the goat's horns.

3. Connect the shapes and erase your guidelines. Add details for the eyes, teeth, a ears. Add texture to the snake-tail. Use short lines to show fur.

# MEDUSA

Medusa was once a beautiful girl. She was so vain that Minerva, the goddess of wisdom, changed Medusa's beautiful hair into snakes. Whenever Medusa looked at people, they would turn to stone!

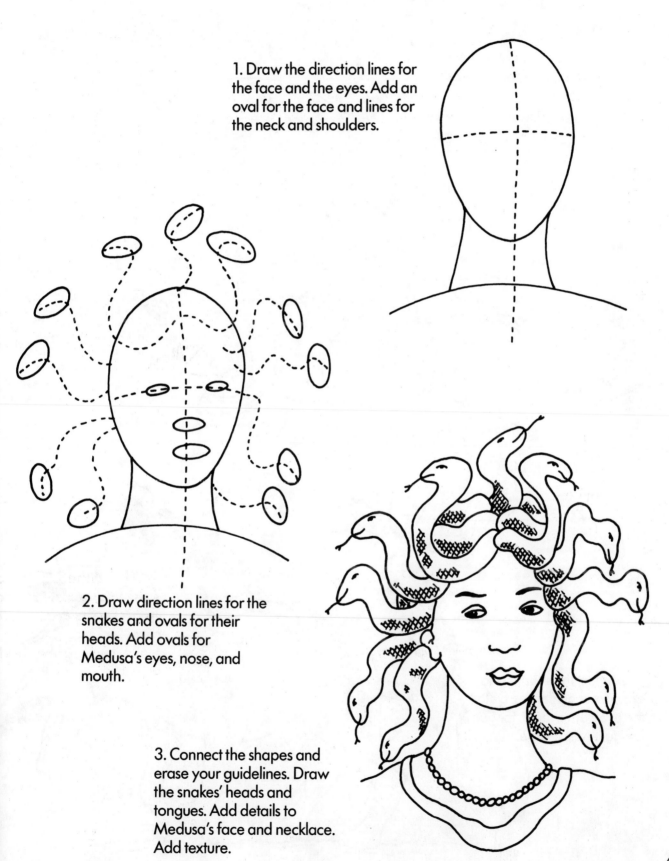

1. Draw the direction lines for the face and the eyes. Add an oval for the face and lines for the neck and shoulders.

2. Draw direction lines for the snakes and ovals for their heads. Add ovals for Medusa's eyes, nose, and mouth.

3. Connect the shapes and erase your guidelines. Draw the snakes' heads and tongues. Add details to Medusa's face and necklace. Add texture.

# CERBERUS

Cerberus was a snarling three-headed watchdog in Greek myth that was supposed to guard the gates of Hell. It had a snake's head on the end of its tail.

1. Draw the direction lines. Add two ovals for the body.

2. Add ovals for the heads, necks, and legs. Draw two lines and an oval for the snake-tail.

3. Connect the shapes and erase your guidelines. Detail the eyes, ears, teeth, tongues, and tail. Add texture.